WORLD HISTORY

China Since World War II

Michael V. Uschan

LUCENT BOOKS
An imprint of Thomson Gale, a part of The Thomson Corporation

GALE
CENGAGE Learning

Detroit • New York • San Francisco • New Haven, Conn • Waterville, Maine • London

LIBRARY OF CONGRESS CATALOGING-IN-PUBLICATION DATA

Uschan, Michael V., 1948–
  China since WW II / by Michael V. Uschan.
     p. cm. — (World history)
  Includes bibliographical references and index.
  ISBN 978-1-4205-0097-4 (hardcover)
  1. China--History--1949---Textbooks. I. Title.
  DS777.55.U75 2009
  951.05--dc22   2008014727

Lucent Books
27500 Drake Rd.
Farmington Hills, MI 48331

ISBN-13: 978-1-4205-0097-4
ISBN-10: 1-4205-0097-4

Printed in the United States of America
2 3 4 5 6 7 12 11 10 09

Contents

Foreword

Each year, on the first day of school, nearly every history teacher faces the task of explaining why his or her students should study history. Many reasons have been given. One is that lessons exist in the past from which contemporary society can benefit and learn. Another is that exploration of the past allows us to see the origins of our customs, ideas, and institutions. Concepts such as democracy, ethnic conflict, or even things as trivial as fashion or mores, have historical roots.

Reasons such as these impress few students, however. If anything, these explanations seem remote and dull to young minds. Yet history is anything but dull. And therein lies what is perhaps the most compelling reason for studying history: History is filled with great stories. The classic themes of literature and drama—love and sacrifice, hatred and revenge, injustice and betrayal, adversity and overcoming adversity—fill the pages of history books, feeding the imagination as well as any of the great works of fiction do.

The story of the Children's Crusade, for example, is one of the most tragic in history. In 1212 Crusader fever hit Europe. A call went out from the pope that all good Christians should journey to Jerusalem to drive out the hated Muslims and return the city to Christian control. Heeding the call, thousands of children made the journey. Parents bravely allowed many children to go, and entire communities were inspired by the faith of these small Crusaders. Unfortunately, many boarded ships captained by slave traders, who enthusiastically sold the children into slavery as soon as they arrived at their destination. Thousands died from disease, exposure, and starvation on the long march across Europe to the Mediterranean Sea. Others perished at sea.

Another story, from a modern and more familiar place, offers a soul-wrenching view of personal humiliation but also the ability to rise above it. Hatsuye Egami was one of 110,000 Japanese Americans sent to internment camps during World War II. "Since yesterday we Japanese have ceased to be human beings," he wrote in his diary. "We are numbers. We are no longer Egamis, but the number 23324. A tag with that number is on every trunk, suitcase and bag. Tags, also, on our breasts." Despite such dehumanizing treatment, most internees worked hard to control their bitterness. They created workable communities inside the camps and demonstrated again and again their loyalty as Americans.

These are but two of the many stories from history that can be found in the pages of the Lucent Books World History series. All World History titles rely on sound research and verifiable evidence, and all give students a clear sense of time, place, and chronology through maps and timelines as well as text.

All titles include a wide range of authoritative perspectives that demonstrate the complexity of historical interpretation and sharpen the reader's critical thinking skills. Formally documented quotations and annotated bibliographies enable students to locate and evaluate sources, often instantaneously via the Internet, and serve as valuable tools for further research and debate.

Finally, Lucent's World History titles present rousing good stories, featuring vivid primary source quotations drawn from unique, sometimes obscure sources such as diaries, public records, and contemporary chronicles. In this way, the voices of participants and witnesses as well as important biographers and historians bring the study of history to life. As we are caught up in the lives of others, we are reminded that we too are characters in the ongoing human saga, and we are better prepared for our own roles.

1945
World War II ends and the Cold War begins; it is a period of heightened tension and rivalry between Communist and democratic nations and lasts nearly five decades.

1954
The U.S. Supreme Court declares racial segregation unconstitutional in *Brown v. Board of Education*.

1958
The Great Leap Forward economic policies begin.

1964
On October 16 China explodes a nuclear bomb in the Gobi Desert.

1947
India gains independence from Great Britain.

1950
Blacks in Johannesburg, South Africa, protest apartheid.

1967
Israeli forces defeat several Arab nations in the Six-Day War.

1945   **1950**   **1960**

1949
Mao Zedong declares the founding of the People's Republic of China (PRC) on October 1.

1950–1953
Between June 25, 1950, and July 27, 1953, the Cold War flares into real war during the Korean War as the PRC and North Korea battle South Korea, the United States, and the forces of the United Nations.

1964–1973
The United States and South Vietnam battle Communist North Vietnam in the Vietnam War.

1966
The Great Proletarian Cultural Revolution begins.

1971
The PRC is admitted to the United Nations on October 25.

1972
U.S. president Richard M. Nixon visits China and meets with Mao on February 27.

1975
In January Zhou Enlai introduces the ideas behind the Four Modernizations.

1984
On December 19 China and Great Britain sign an agreement returning Hong Kong and other territory to China.

1986
A Soviet nuclear reactor in Chernobyl explodes.

1990
The Human Genome Project is launched. In South Africa, antiapartheid leader Nelson Mandela is released from prison after twenty-seven years of confinement.

2006
China completes construction of the Three Gorges Dam.

1970   1980   1990   2000

1978
Leaders of Israel and Egypt meet at Camp David with U.S. president Jimmy Carter and reach a peace settlement. In the PRC, Deng Xiaoping begins introducing changes in the economy that will make life better for most Chinese people.

1979
China and the United States resume normal diplomatic relations on January 1. On January 28, Deng Xiaoping visits the United States.

1989
The Berlin Wall is torn down. Between April 15 and June 4, China experiences democracy protests and the Tiananmen Square Massacre.

2001
The United States is attacked by terrorists on September 11. In Uganda, the ebola virus breaks out, killing hundreds of people.

1997
On July 1 China gets back Hong Kong and other territory from Great Britain.

1994
Conflict between the Tutsi and Hutu ethnic groups in Rwanda results in the deaths of some five hundred thousand people.

2008
Violence flares in Tibet as citizens demand more freedom. Between August 8 and 24, China hosts the Summer Olympics.

China's Continuing Revolution

There are two main types of revolutions. One revolution is the use of military force to seize political control of a country. However, a revolution can also occur when a nation's political leaders make major, fundamental changes in the economic or social rules by which they govern their nation. Since World War II ended in 1945, a series of both types of revolution have dramatically changed China. The most significant revolution was the Chinese Communist Party's (CCP) victory in a long, bloody civil war for political control of China.

Mao Zedong was the military and political leader most responsible for the triumph that allowed the CCP to establish the People's Republic of China (PRC) on October 1, 1949. For the next three decades, Mao used his dictatorial power to force other revolutions upon the world's most populous nation. Mao explained in January 1958 why it was important to keep the spirit of revolution alive: "Continuing revolution. Our revolutions come one after another. [Our] revolutions are like battles. After a victory [in one revolution], we must at once put forward a new task. In this way, cadres [government and party officials] and the masses will forever be filled with revolutionary fervor."[1]

Revolutions continued to alter China after Mao's death in 1976 because leaders like Deng Xiaoping continued to foster dramatic changes in China's economic, political, and social structures. Some of the revolutions Mao and other leaders started were misguided and harmful. Taken as a whole, however, they have improved life for the Chinese people and have helped China become one of the world's most powerful countries.

A Communist Revolution

In 1949 Mao was asked what he would do to make life better for the nation's

550 million people. Mao had a simple response: "How do we change [China]? The country must be destroyed and then re-formed."[2] Mao transformed China by replacing its political and economic systems with Communism, a totalitarian form of government in which the state wields supreme power over its citizens.

Communism is also an economic system in which the state, and not individuals, owns and controls land,

Mao Zedong transformed China by replacing its political and economic systems with Communism.

businesses, and industries. The most dramatic economic change was in rural areas, where 80 percent of China's people lived. The Communists seized land from wealthy individuals and distributed it to poor families so they could grow enough food to feed themselves. Sociologist C.K. Yang claims this change was historic: "Land reform was one of the most momentous events in the history of China. When the entire process had been concluded for the nation as a whole, some 700 million mu [more than 100 million acres] of land had been distributed to 300 million landless or land-short peasants."[3]

This change helped many people have a better life. However, in 1958 Mao began forcing farmers to give up

their land to create much larger farms, called communes, so they could work together to grow crops. Communes were designed to increase food production to feed China's rapidly growing population, but the change proved to be disastrous: China's crops decreased so much that in the early 1960s millions of people died of starvation.

Mao wielded so much power that other leaders could not radically change the agricultural system until after he died in 1976. New leader Deng Xiaoping then allowed farmers to own land again. He also made other revolutionary changes to strengthen the nation's economy, such as allowing people to own businesses, and he permitted foreign nations to open industries in China.

Deng's policies produced more food and created so many good jobs that people were able to live decent lives. As a farmer in a rural community in Sichuan Province explained in the 1980s, "We owe our liberation to Chairman Mao and our prosperity to Deng Xiaoping."[4] Even though Deng's policies violated Communist beliefs, his successors continued them because they were so successful. Deng and other leaders, however, refused to surrender the complete control they had over their citizens.

Little Freedom in China

The Communists forced everyone to accept their political theories and government policies and punished anyone who opposed them by imprisoning them or killing them. Despite that, many Chinese by the 1960s were losing faith in Communism and were demanding more personal freedom. This angered Mao, who in 1966 began encouraging young people to band together in Red Guard units to criticize anyone who strayed from Communist doctrine. "Liberate the little ones!" Mao said. "I shall call for rebellion in the provinces."[5]

What became known as the Cultural Revolution backfired when it led to several years of violence against millions of people, including many high-ranking Communist officials. Instead of only criticizing people for rejecting Communism, Red Guards and their supporters beat and murdered them. The ensuing chaos the Cultural Revolution caused for nearly a decade ruined the lives of millions of Chinese people as it resulted in the deaths of thousands of people, widespread destruction of homes and buildings, and a weaker economy.

Although Chinese leaders after Mao realized the Cultural Revolution had been a mistake, they continued to repress political freedom so no one could challenge their power. In the spring of 1989, students and other people throughout China staged protests to demand more freedom. The government responded with a brutal crackdown on protesters that culminated in June with the Tiananmen Square Massacre in Beijing. Hundreds and perhaps thousands of people—no exact figures are known—were wounded or killed when military units moved people out of the historic square.

The government brutality ended the dissent. It also showed the world that China still refused to allow its people real freedom.

Still Little Freedom

On October 1, 2007, the fifty-eighth anniversary of the founding of the PRC, Chinese premier Wen Jiabao praised China's economic growth since Deng and noted that it had "remarkably improved the people's living standard."[6] In just a few decades, China had been transformed from a nation in which most people had trouble making enough money to survive to one in which some people had become millionaires and most had enough money to own things like television sets and computers.

But Chinese officials were still trying to control what they thought and said. One way they did that was to punish people who started or visited Internet sites that criticized the government. Hao Wu started a site called "Beijing or Bust" that was mildly critical of the government. In 2006 the Chinese government imprisoned Hao for 140 days for writing about religious discrimination against Chinese Christians. After his release, Hao jokingly blogged about his arrest: "I'm not one of those who fight to break the shackles. But I can dance. Dance with my shackles. Dance with my bondage after the shackles."[7]

Chapter One

The Communists Conquer China

In the fall of 1949 the Chinese Communist Party was on the verge of victory in the civil war for control of China. On September 21 CCP chairman Mao Zedong hosted a meeting in Beijing of high-ranking party officials and civilians from various business, labor, and cultural groups. The goal of the meeting was to refine plans on how to govern China when the fighting ended. Mao told members of the Chinese People's Political Consultative Conference that they should be proud of what they had done to help win the long, bloody struggle:

> Fellow Delegates, we are all convinced that our work will go down in the history of mankind, demonstrating that the Chinese people, comprising one quarter of humanity, have now stood up. [For] over a century our forefathers never stopped waging un-yielding struggles against domestic and foreign oppressors. . . . Ours will no longer be a nation subject to insult and humiliation. We have stood up![8]

Mao believed the military conquest he had directed was more than just a triumph for Communism. He considered it vindication for average Chinese people, who for thousands of years had been dominated by a small elite of wealthy and powerful people that included emperors and empresses. He believed it was a warning to the United States and other foreign countries that China was now strong enough to stop them from bullying it economically and politically. Mao also saw it as the end of a struggle of more than one hundred years by Chinese people to feel proud again of their once powerful nation, which had grown weak during that period compared with other countries.

Chairman Mao, speaking in Tiananmen Square, proclaims the establishment of the People's Republic of China on October 1, 1949.

Ten days later, on October 1, Mao spoke at a more public celebration of the CCP victory when he triumphantly entered Beijing's Tiananmen Square to announce the establishment of the People's Republic of China (PRC). Along with other Communist officials, Mao stood atop the massive Tiananmen Gate that dominated the square so people in the vast crowd of more than one hundred thousand could see him deliver the speech. When spectators began shouting, "Long live Chairman Mao!" he responded gleefully by saying, "Long live the people!"[9]

It was symbolic for Mao to announce the new Chinese nation from Tiananmen, which in Chinese means "Gate of

Heavenly Peace." Tiananmen was one of several entrances to the Forbidden City, a vast complex of nearly one thousand buildings in Beijing that housed the royal family that had ruled China for more than six hundred years.

An Ancient but Weak Nation

Founded more than five thousand years ago, China is one of the world's oldest civilizations. Written records for some of the cultures that have flourished in China date back nearly thirty-five hundred years. China was ruled for thousands of years by various royal families known as dynasties. One of the most famous dynasties was that of Emperor Zheng, who established the Qin dynasty. China's name was devised from Zheng's dynastic name because Qin in English is pronounced "chin."

For thousands of years, China was the dominant country in Asia as well as one of the most innovative in the world. China invented paper, the compass, gunpowder, and printing before other nations, and its written language has been in continuous use longer than any other system of writing. By the beginning of the twentieth century, however, China was weak compared with other nations in terms of economic, political, and military strength. China's status had diminished because of the inability of the Qing dynasty, the royal family that had been in power since 1644, to govern the nation.

Confusion over Written Chinese

Peking or Beijing? Mao Tse-tung or Mao Zedong? Chiang Kai-shek or Jiang Jieshi? Actually, both spellings for the names of China's capital city and two of the most influential figures in China during the twentieth century are correct. Although Western nations use letters of the Roman alphabet to build words, written Chinese consists of thousands of characters that stand for entire words. When people from Western nations began trying to transcribe spoken Mandarin, China's official language, they had to invent a system to translate the characters into Roman letters. The first spelling in all three examples adheres to the Wade-Giles system, which was commonly accepted around the world in the nineteenth century; the second spelling of the names is in Hanyu pinyin. The People's Republic of China created pinyin because they believed it was a more accurate way for Westerners to write spoken Mandarin. After China officially adopted pinyin in 1979, most countries began using it instead of Wade-Giles. There is still some confusion about which spelling is correct because some older books and other sources for information on China still use the older system.

China had also grown backward and uneducated compared with many other countries because Qing emperors in the nineteenth century rejected new ideas and technologies that Europeans brought to China. However, some people in China wanted to adopt these new ideas. In 1842 Wei Yuan, a scholar, recommended "building ships [like those Europeans had], making [modern] weapons, and learning the superior techniques of the barbarians."[10] Yuan's comment came shortly after Great Britain used its military power to force China to allow it to continue selling opium even though the emperor had banned the drug. In the second half of the nineteenth century, other nations, including Russia and Japan, also forced China to give them economic concessions. The nation's weakness humiliated Chinese citizens and turned them against the Qing dynasty.

The Qing dynasty also lost support because of the deplorable conditions under which most people lived. While a small elite composed of royalty and wealthy landowners and businessmen enjoyed luxurious lifestyles, the vast majority of people were poor and lived on the edge of starvation. In 1903 Zou Rong, an eighteen-year-old student, criticized the Qing in a book called *The Revolutionary Army*. Zou wrote, "I do not begrudge repeating over and over again that we are the slaves of the [Qing] and suffering from their tyranny."[11]

In 1903 China was ruled by Empress Cixi, who was the most powerful royal figure in China from 1861 until her death in 1908. On December 2, 1908, her successor was her two-year-old nephew Pu Yi, who was destined to be the last Chinese emperor.

The Republic of China

The Qing dynasty survived several attempts to overthrow it in the second half of the nineteenth century, but it finally fell during the 1911 Rebellion, which began on October 10, 1911. Soldiers in Wuchang started the rebellion and were soon joined by students and other people who demanded a better form of government. Leaders of various political groups banded together to force the emperor to surrender his hereditary authority over China. On January 1, 1912, this political coalition established the Republic of China and named Sun Yat-sen its provisional president.

Sun, a medical doctor, was a member of the Guomindang (People's National) Party. He had learned about democracy while living for several years in Honolulu, Hawaii, with his brother, and he wanted the republic to be a democracy. His dream for that died when former Qing general Yuan Shikai seized power and became president. Yuan's rule was brief—he died on June 6, 1916—and weak because he never had enough military might to unite the vast country. For more than a decade after his death warlords who commanded their own private armies ruled various areas of China while vying to win control of the entire nation.

China remained locked in this military and political struggle for several years. Then, on March 4, 1919, students in Beijing staged a massive protest march in Tiananmen Square. Their demands for better government made people throughout the country think about how China could overcome its problems. During this period Lu Hsun, a famous novelist, wrote many books about China's future. In one of them, he posed a question that he said every Chinese person had to answer: "Vast territory, abundant resources, and a great population—with such excellent material are we able only to go round and round in circles?"[12]

Many people began trying to answer that important question. Within a decade, two groups with contrasting political philosophies and ideas on how to effectively govern China were locked in a bitter civil war—the Guomindang and the CCP.

Nationalists and Communists

After Yuan died, Sun tried to strengthen the Guomindang by seeking support from foreign nations. The only country that offered help was the Union of Soviet Socialist Republics (USSR). The Soviet Union had been known as Russia until Communists seized power from the Russian royal family during World War I. In 1923 the Soviets began providing the Guomindang funds to train and equip an army so it could defeat the warlords and unite China. Two years earlier, however, the Soviets had helped found the CCP. Even though they were rivals, the two parties began working together to unify China.

Sun died on March 12, 1925. He was succeeded by Chiang Kai-shek, a military leader who, from 1926 to 1928, successfully led Guomindang troops to victory over warlords who controlled most of China. Chiang had studied

Sun Yat-Sen was named the first president of the Republic of China on January 1, 1912.

military and political ideas in Moscow for several months and willingly worked with Communists. But in April 1927, after Communists helped his troops capture Shanghai, he turned against them because he wanted to wield power himself. Vowing that he would not rest "until every Red [Communist] soldier in China is exterminated and every Communist is in prison,"[13] Chiang outlawed the CCP and declared all Communists criminals. He purged Communist officials in the Guomindang government and arrested and murdered thousands more throughout China.

One of the Communists Chiang sought for extermination was Mao, who was born on December 26, 1893, in Shaoshan, a small village in which his father owned enough land to be modestly rich. In 1910 Mao read *Words of Warning to an Affluent Age*, a book that affected him so deeply that he never forgot its opening sentence: "Alas, China will be subjugated!" He said learning how weak China was in comparison with other nations had made him "realize that it was the duty of all the people to help save it."[14] He dedicated his life to making China strong again.

In the summer of 1920, Mao helped establish the CCP. Mao became a Communist because he believed the wealthy elite that ruled China was abusing the vast majority of Chinese people, especially those living in rural areas. In a report Mao wrote in 1927, he claimed that rural Chinese were the key to victory for a Communist revolution: "This leadership of the poor peasants is ab-solutely necessary. Without the poor peasants there can be no revolution. To reject them is to reject the revolution. To attack them is to attack the revolution. Their general direction of the revolution has never been wrong."[15]

When Chiang declared war on the Communists, they fled to rural areas because the Guomindang controlled most cities. The support Communists received from rural Chinese would help them defeat the Guomindang and make Mao's prediction about their importance come true.

The Long March

Chiang established his Guomindang government in Nanjing while the Communists created the Chinese Soviet Republic in southeastern Jianxi Province. During the next few years Chiang dispatched large armies to destroy the Communists, but troops led by Mao defeated them every time. After Chiang turned against the Communists, Mao had decided that military might was necessary for his party's survival. Claiming that Chiang "rose [to power] by grasping the gun," Mao claimed that "from now on, we should pay the greatest attention to military affairs. We must know that political power is obtained from the barrel of the gun."[16]

Even Mao's able leadership, however, could not stop Chiang in 1934, when he gathered a huge force of more than 750,000 soldiers. They surrounded the Communist stronghold and began destroying homes, businesses, and farms while killing hundreds of thou-

In October 1934 Mao Zedong, on horseback, led eighty-six thousand people on a trek that would become known as the Long March.

sands of people in an attempt to eradicate the Communists.

On October 15, 1934, faced with extinction, eighty-six thousand people headed for the safety of another Communist enclave in Shaanxi Province in northwest China. The historic trek for survival known as the Long March covered 6,000 miles (9,656km) and took 368 days. Communist soldiers had to continually fight a rear-guard action against pursuing soldiers to protect the fleeing refugees. The Communists trav-

eled a winding route to evade a superior force that could destroy them. When the journey finally ended a little more than a year later, on October 25, 1935, only about eight thousand people were left alive; the others had died of starvation, disease, or combat wounds. Despite the huge loss of life, the Long March allowed a small remnant of the CCP to survive, and they were soon joined by thousands of new supporters.

The Communists established a community in Yenan. They had escaped

Chiang, but a new, even more powerful threat to their existence soon arose.

World War II

Japan and China had been enemies for centuries. In 1931 Japan seized Manchuria, a northern area of China. Japan renamed the area Manchukuo and named former emperor Pu Yi to head this new nation. China was too weak and divided by its civil war to stop Japan from taking Manchuria. No other country intervened on China's behalf. In 1937 Japan invaded China again. The fighting between Japan and China marked the beginning of World War II, which eventually involved European countries and the United States.

The Communists wanted to work with the Guomindang to oppose Japan, but Chiang hated them so much that he refused. Guomindang leaders were so disgusted that Chiang seemed unwilling to defend China that on December 12, 1936, they kidnapped him. When Chiang protested, "I'm your commander-in-chief," one of the soldiers who seized him responded, "Yes, but you are also our prisoner."[17] Chiang's captors flew him to a meeting with Communist leader Zhou Enlai in Sian, where Chiang was forced to agree to help defend China.

The Importance of the Long March

The Long March that allowed several thousand Communists to escape Guomindang (National People's) Party forces in 1934 and 1935 is one of the most legendary feats of the Communist revolution. In December 1935, two months after the march ended, Mao Zedong explained why it was important:

For twelve months we were under daily reconnaissance and bombing from the air by scores of planes. We were encircled, pursued, obstructed and intercepted on the ground by a big force of several hundred thousand men. We encountered untold difficulties and great obstacles on the way, but by keeping our two feet going we swept across a distance of more than [6,000 miles (9,656km)] through the length and breadth of eleven provinces. Well, has there ever been in history a long march like ours? No, never. The Long March is also a manifesto [political statement]. It proclaims to the world that the Red Army is an army of heroes. [It also] declares to the two hundred million people of eleven provinces that only the road of the Red Army leads to their liberation.

Quoted in David Sylvester et al., *The Rise of Communist China.* St. Paul, MN: Greenhaven, 1979, p. 29.

The Communists used Mao's military tactics to effectively fight the Japanese invaders. Chiang, however, never launched an effective counteroffensive even though he received weapons and other supplies from the United States. Historians believe Chiang did not want to weaken his army against the Japanese because he knew he would have to fight the Communists when the war ended. U.S. lieutenant general Joseph Stilwell helped direct the Chinese war effort. He claimed the Communists were better fighters than the Guomindang: "These Reds may be bandits but bandits or not they're masters of guerrilla warfare. [It] looks like they've got the kind of leaders who win."[18]

Stilwell praised the Communists' fighting skills even though the United States officially opposed Communism. Stilwell's comment on Communist fighting efficiency proved prophetic when civil war flared anew in China. After Japan surrendered on August 15, 1945, to end World War II, the Communists and the Guomindang resumed fighting.

Civil War Again

Most people had believed the Guomindang would triumph when they began battling again. Chiang had three times as many soldiers, and his army was better equipped thanks to the United States, which gave him $5 billion in military aid as part of its postwar crusade against Communism. But the Communists had done something during World War II that the world did not know about—they had won the hearts and minds of millions of people in China —and this hidden strength helped them defeat the Guomindang.

In 1945 about 110 million people lived in areas controlled by Communists, which was only one-third the number of people Chiang governed. Most people living in Communist areas had a better life than those in Guomindang territory. The Guomindang was a military dictatorship. It ignored the plight of poor people who made up the majority of China's citizens. Meanwhile, the Communists fed their citizens, opened schools and hospitals, and treated them with respect. For example, Chiang's soldiers often stole food from peasants or forced them to work as slave laborers. "They demand such and such amounts of food, and never a word about payment,"[19] complained one Chinese farmer. Communists, by contrast, paid for everything they needed. They were especially popular in rural areas, where they gave peasants land they seized from the rich so the poor farmers could grow enough food to feed their families.

More Chinese began to support the Communists because they believed they would give them a better life than the Guomindang. As a result, by 1949 the Communist People's Liberation Army (PLA) had grown to 4 million soldiers, nearly three times that of the Guomindang. This superiority enabled Mao to back up the vow he made on October 17, 1945, before both sides had resumed fighting: "If they [the

The Communists Lived in Caves

When the Communists established their headquarters in Yenan in 1936, they lived in crude caves like poor people there always had. Historian Jonathan D. Spence claims the simple lifestyle Communists adopted made local people respect them:

By the fall of 1936 the Communists had decided to make their headquarters in [Yenan], a fair sized market town with good shelter nearby in the cave dwellings that peasants for centuries had built into the soft hillsides. Such dwellings were cheap to build and gave good protection from the extremes of heat and cold that afflicted this arid region. And in a country almost barren of trees, the need for timber was reduced to some simple framing for a rough screen and door that would shelter the cave dwellers from wind, dust, and the gaze of the outside world. The fact that Mao [Zedong] lived in such a cave struck visitors as symbolic of his revolutionary simplicity and fervor. In fact, it was an adjustment to circumstances, of a kind he had made many times before in his life, and Mao settled at once into this strangely desolate new home.

Jonathan D. Spence, *Mao Zedong*. New York: Penguin Putnam, 1999, p. 87.

A family poses for a photograph outside their cave dwelling near Yenan in 1935. Thousands of Chinese were living in caves.

Guomindang] fight, we will wipe them out completely."[20] The PLA's superior size and military leadership enabled the Communists to win control of more and more territory, and by the time the Communists captured Beijing in January 1949 their victory was inevitable. The Communists then kept pushing south to occupy the Guomindang capital of Nanjing on April 21, Wuhan on May 17, Sian on May 20, and Shanghai on May 27 while forcing Chiang's forces to flee before them.

On December 10 Communist soldiers laid siege to Chengdu, the last Guomindang-occupied city in China. Realizing he had been defeated, on December 10 Chiang fled for Taiwan, an island off China's coast. An estimated 2 million Guomindang soldiers and civilians also went to Taiwan. Chiang, claiming he was still the rightful ruler of China, declared the island to be the new home of the Republic of China (ROC). (To avoid confusion between the two nations claiming to be China, the PRC is sometimes referred to as *mainland China* whereas the ROC is usually called *Taiwan*.)

Chiang promised to one day come back and defeat the Communists. The real ruler of China now, however, was Mao.

A Communist Emperor

Mao was jubilant when Communist troops captured Beijing, the historic seat of power for Chinese rulers. Mao even joked, "As soon as we enter Beijing, I'll be an emperor, won't I?"[21] Although Mao would only have the title of "chairman" of the Chinese Communist Party, he would wield as much power over China as any emperor ever had.

Chapter Two

China Becomes a Communist Nation

Some changes the Communist Party made in the new People's Republic of China were easy. They picked Beijing as China's capital, agreed on a national flag that was red with five yellow stars, and chose "The March of the Volunteers" as a national anthem. It was much more difficult to put into effect the drastic political, economic, and social changes that would turn China into a Communist state. Mao Zedong, however, had always known that such a revolutionary transformation of his homeland would not be easy. In 1927 Mao explained that creating true revolution was difficult as well as violent: "A revolution is not a dinner party, or writing an essay, or painting a picture, or doing embroidery; it cannot be so refined, so leisurely and gentle, so temperate, kind, courteous, restrained and magnanimous. A revolution is an insurrection, an act of violence by which one class overthrows another."[22]

The first Communist revolution was the military overthrow of the Guomindang government. The second Communist revolution entailed changing nearly every aspect of the daily lives of the nation's 550 million people. In some cases, this revolution was as violent as the first.

A Gradual Transition to Communism

The CCP is the only political party allowed in China and has complete authority to govern the nation. CCP officials appoint public officials at every level of government—party members always hold the most important positions—and decide public policy. This one-party rule is actually similar to that of the Guomindang Party, which was a military dictatorship. The National People's Congress (NPC) is made up of more than two thousand party members who represent every area of China; they are elected by other party members and not the general public. True power is held by a small group of national leaders who are members of the PRC's Politburo Standing Committee. Mao was the first chairman of this committee, which made him China's most powerful official.

Although the Communists had the power to immediately turn China into a Communist society, they decided to do it gradually to give people time to recover from two decades of warfare. Mao himself explained, "China needs a period of three-to-five years of peace, which would be used to bring the economy back to pre-war levels and to stabilize the country in general."[23] The Communists began their rule by dividing China into six military regions and appointing officials to oversee various areas.

The CCP allowed many former Guomindang local officials to continue in their positions because they knew how

These women working outside of a church were part of the Family Home Organization, which worked to improve sanitary conditions in their local community.

to meet the needs of citizens. However-er, the Communists also formed small groups that worked to improve living conditions in their neighborhoods. A woman who was a member of one of the Family Women's Organizations that started in every community explained how workers would improve sanita-tion: "We'll get some powdered lime to sprinkle around the sewer drains [and] we've already contracted with plumb-ers to clean the drains twice a month. Besides cleaning up all the places where rats can nest, we should use traps and bait to catch them."[24]

The fact that women did such work and were placed in positions of author-ity was one major change the Commu-nists made immediately. In the past, women had been considered inferior to men. This attitude was summed up in a saying by the revered philosopher Confucius: "Women are human, but lower than men [and should] not be al-lowed any will of their own."[25] But the Communists considered women equal to men, and Liao Lixiu was grateful for the new freedom women had: "In the old society we country women dared not go out [of the house]. We didn't go to plays or theaters or even to the mar-ket. Now that the liberation had come no wonder all of us women were hap-py! We liked it. We came out. How we hated those who held us down!"[26]

The Communists instituted other positive social changes, such as banning the sale of opium and other drugs, pros-titution, and gambling. They also out-lawed slavery. Before the Communist takeover, poor people sometimes had to sell one of their children to buy food so the rest of the family could survive. And adults could be forced into slavery if they could not pay back loans from rich people. The Communists also helped poor people become educated. In 1949 most Chinese were illiterate because they were too poor to attend school. The PRC began a free school system, and by 1952 about 60 percent of children were attending class; more people also began attending universities.

The most dramatic change the Com-munists made in the first three years of their rule was in rural China. Commu-nists transformed life there by giving more people land to farm.

Land Reform and a Communist Economy

The main reason the Communists gained enough support to defeat the Guomindang was the income disparity that existed between the small elite that controlled the bulk of China's wealth and the majority of people who were poor. This contrast was most glaring in rural areas, where a handful of rich people owned almost all the farmland. Many peasants rented land to grow food, but the rent they paid was often so high that they lived on the edge of starvation. The Communist land re-form program seized 45 percent of Chi-na's farmland from landlords—people who made money from renting land— and gave it to the nearly 70 percent of rural residents who had little or no land. The land enabled poor peasants

Women Had New Freedom

The People's Republic of China gave women something they had never had before—equality with men. The republic's Common Program guaranteed that "in political, economic, cultural, educational and social aspects of life women possess equal rights and privileges with men. Freedom of marriage is adopted for both men and women." In the past, parents usually chose the men that women married. On Women's Day, March 8, 1951, a newspaper editorial exhorted women to learn to be strong:

We must remold ourselves in order that we may survive in and not be washed away by the current of this great age. To meet the demands of the social situation, we must learn to make progress and overcome our own weaknesses. Most of us do not have interest or confidence in political study; we even let household duties prevent us from thinking and learning, confining our views only to our husbands and children to the exclusion of everything else. We must have determination to overcome such weakness."

Quoted in C.K. Yang, *The Chinese Family in the Communist Revolution*. Cambridge, MA: Technology, 1959, pp. 122–23.

to grow enough food to survive. The Communists also gave the landlords' livestock to the poor.

The CCP allowed residents of each Chinese village to divide up land themselves. This process began with a public hearing in which people criticized landlords, who were considered criminals for having profited at the expense of other people. In Shanxi village, the wife of peasant Li Mao complained about landlord Sheng Jinghe: "Once I went to glean wheat on your land. But you cursed me and drove me away. Why did you curse and beat me? And why did you seize the wheat I had gleaned?"[27] Gleaning occurs when people try to recover a few grains of wheat from fields that have already been harvested. The landlord had not allowed the hungry woman to do even that.

Peasants hated landlords so much that they beat and sometimes killed them during the land reform period from 1949 to 1952. In the same period, Communists hunted down and punished counter-revolutionaries—people who opposed Communism. This group included former Guomindang leaders, rich businessmen, some intellectuals, and Chinese employees of foreign-owned companies. Historians believe that Communists killed as many as 20 million landlords and revolutionaries. Mao claimed that such violence was necessary: "Whom have we executed? What sort of people? Elements for whom the masses had great hatred. If we did not kill some tyrants, or if we were too lenient to them, the masses would not agree [with Communist policies.]"[28]

This far-reaching economic reform took place in nearly 1 million villages. The Communists also made changes to China's economy in urban areas, but they were not as severe. Although the PRC assumed ownership of all banks and most businesses, it allowed some individuals to continue owning and operating factories and industrial enterprises. The PRC also began directing reconstruction of war damage to the nation's roads, railroad lines, and buildings.

To rebuild its shattered nation and economy, China needed financial assistance. It got it from the Union of Soviet Socialist Republics (USSR).

A Communist Economy

China turned to the Soviet Union for help because the United States, Great

In 1952 Communists began executing Guomintang leaders, counterrevolutionaries and rich businessmen. In the end some 20 million died as Mao proclaimed it was necessary to control the people.

Britain, and other rich nations all opposed Communism. In December 1949 Mao made his first trip outside of China when he went to Moscow, Russia, to meet with Soviet dictator Joseph Stalin. The two worked out the Treaty of Alliance and Mutual Assistance in which the Soviets gave China $300 million in aid. The Soviets also agreed to send thousands of military, scientific, and technological experts to help modernize China's industry and armed forces. The two countries also pledged to come to each other's aid if they were attacked by another nation.

By 1952 China's recovery from years of warfare had strengthened the nation enough to make Mao believe it was time to complete the economic transformation of China into a Communist state. China decided to pattern the Chinese economy after the USSR's model. Under the Soviet model, the state owned all businesses and industries, and agriculture was performed by large units instead of individual farmers. The Soviets also depended on a small group of economic experts to plan the nation's entire economy in five-year time periods.

The PRC initiated the Soviet model in its First Five-Year Plan, which ran from 1953 through 1957. The PRC seized control of all major industries and businesses and used centralized planning to formulate goals for each segment of the economy. During this period China was able to increase production of iron, steel, and other key commodities. That was partly due to the expertise of Soviet advisers, who helped the Chinese build and operate hundreds of new plants.

China also harvested larger crops of rice, wheat, and other food it badly needed to feed its growing population. The food increase was partially due to the formation of hundreds of thousands of cooperatives throughout China. In these agricultural partnerships, twenty or more farm families banded together so they could farm more land more efficiently. Crops they raised were divided among the cooperative members according to formulas based on how much land and labor each family had contributed.

The five-year plan benefited almost everyone. But because some farmers were still making a profit, Mao began to fear the Chinese were reverting to capitalism. As early as July 31, 1955, Mao claimed in a speech that "new rich [farmers] have sprung up everywhere. If this tendency goes unchecked, the separation into two extremes in the countryside will get worse day by day."[29] This concern, and Mao's belief that China needed to undergo perpetual revolution to stay strong, led him to believe it was time to make even more radical changes in China. Mao had expressed this in 1948 when he said, "We cannot go on consolidating [a social system] for all time, otherwise we will make inflexible the ideology reflecting this system and render people incapable of adjusting their thoughts to new changes."[30]

Mao's thinking laid the groundwork for the Second Five-Year Plan

An Agricultural Cooperative

In 1955 about twenty farm families in MaGaoqiao, a small community in Sichuan Province, banded together into a cooperative. Wu Zhengfu explains why the cooperative farming was a good idea:

We understood co-operation as the way to get all the people rich together. It is a way to avoid two extremes—the rich and the poor. As for farm production, some peasants are skilled and some are not, so through the co-operative the skillful ones could help the others. They said the way of the collective would be stronger for fighting natural disasters and for improving the farming environment. [After] the co-operative was set up, we worked together on our fields. We did our production quite well. For the first year we distributed the resulting income according to a principle of seven parts to three parts. Three parts according to our land shares and seven parts according to our labor. Many people felt encouraged by our activity and sooner or later more applied to join.

Quoted in Stephen Endicott, *Red Earth: Revolution in a Sichuan Village.* New York: New Amsterdam, 1991, p. 53.

(1958– 1962). It was dubbed "the Great Leap Forward," and it would lead the PRC into the most severe domestic crisis in its history.

The Great Leap

The radical economic changes Mao proposed were partially due to his impatience in making China's economy one of the world's most powerful. He dreamed that China, in just a few more years, could begin producing more key products, such as steel, than Western nations like Great Britain. He believed that all China needed to do was to mobilize its workforce in new ways. Under a rallying cry of "More, better, faster, cheaper!"[31] the CCP began to reshape the nation's basic economic structure.

The most drastic change was in agriculture. Between April and September 1958, more than 90 percent of all farm households were forced to join giant state-owned and state-operated communes that averaged about twenty-five thousand people. Unlike the cooperatives, individual farmers had to surrender ownership of their land as well as their livestock, farm equipment, and some personal possessions. Some people stayed in their own homes, but many lived in communal dormitories and ate meals in cafeterias. Most children were now cared for in nurseries because mothers had to work full time. Residents of MaGaoqiao, a small community in Sichuan Province, joined the Junction People's Commune, which had nearly fifty-two hundred families. Wang Daoquan said people liked the commune: "When communization came we thought it was much better. All expenses were covered—food, clothing, medicine, child-delivery, even your haircut—and you still had your wages. It was very good."[32]

Because communes were supposed to make farming more efficient, the CCP shifted 100 million rural workers to jobs in factories, mines, and gigantic public works projects in which they built dams and irrigation systems. To produce more steel, the CCP set up more than seven hundred thousand small backyard foundries in rural and urban areas and forced everyone, even doctors and teachers, to spend their spare time making steel. As many as 90 million people became involved in this steel-making plan.

The Great Leap seemed to be working in 1958, when industrial output increased substantially and there was a plentiful harvest. But during the next three years, the new economic ideas failed miserably and created a disaster of historic proportions.

Famine and Failure

The main problem with the Great Leap was that it misused China's greatest strength—its gigantic labor force—by forcing workers to perform nearly impossible tasks in projects that often failed to accomplish their goals. Workers who built dams were forced to move tons of earth by carrying dirt in baskets on their backs. When one commune wanted to make a farm field drain properly, it had workers use hand tools to carve a quarter-mile (.4km) tunnel beneath the field.

Many projects were poorly thought out and executed. A thousand women and adolescents from the Equality Commune in Guangdong Province worked throughout the winter of 1958 to build dams so a river channel could be diverted to create ponds to raise fish. But a spring flood washed the dams away and killed seven people. Asked about the project years later, a woman who toiled on it claimed, "It was crazy. Everyone knew it [would fail]."[33] The government also sent peasants who had little or no prospecting knowledge into the countryside to hunt for uranium and petroleum. People trying to make steel in their backyards did not know what they were doing. As a result, the metal they made was inferior and much of it was unusable.

The worst misuse of Chinese labor, however, was that so many rural men were taken away to do other jobs that there were not enough farmworkers. This manpower shortage and bad weather in 1959, 1960, and 1961 created a drastic decline in agricultural production. The result was the most widespread famine in China in a century. Journalist Stanley Karnow interviewed people who fled China during this period. This is how he described the situation that existed in 1960: "There was no meat, no fish, scarcely any vegetables, and reduced portions of rice. People spoke of having eaten wild herbs [and] a girl said that peasants ate cakes made from cotton seeds, a form of nourishment normally reserved for pigs."[34]

Historians today estimate that 20 million Chinese died of starvation from 1958 until the early 1960s. Communist officials became aware of the growing disaster but were afraid to criticize the Great Leap because it meant attacking Mao's ideas. But in July 1959 Peng Dehuai dared to call the plans unrealistic at a Communist Party meeting in Lushan. Mao was angry that someone had dared question him, but he accepted responsibility for the failure. On July 23 Mao admitted, "It is I who am to blame."[35]

After that meeting, the CCP retreated from the Great Leap. To increase food production, it forced 25 million city

In 1958 90 percent of all farm households were forced to join state-operated communes like this one in Yunnan province.

Backyard Steel Mills

Perhaps the greatest absurdity of the Great Leap Forward was the decision to have people try to make steel in their backyards. In Mao: The Unknown Story, *authors Jung Chang and Jon Halliday explain how foolish this idea was:*

At least 90 million people were "forced," as Mao said matter-of-factly, to construct such furnaces which produced not steel at all, but [inferior] iron. To feed these furnaces, the population was coerced into donating virtually every piece of metal they had, regardless of whether this was being used in productive, even essential, objects. Farm tools, even water wagons, were carted off and melted down, as were cooking utensils, iron door handles and women's hair clips. Across China yet more peasant houses were torn down, and their occupants made homeless, so that the timber and thatch could be burned as fuel [to melt metal]. Most accessible mountains and hillsides were stripped bare of trees. The resulting deforestation was still causing floods decades later.

Jung Chang and Jon Halliday, *Mao: The Unknown Story*. New York: Knopf, 2004, p. 432.

Many small villages were forced by Mao into building small backyard furnaces that produced a low-grade iron.

dwellers to move to rural areas and become agricultural workers, reduced the size of communes to the more efficient collectives of the early 1950s, and allowed farmers to grow food on privately owned plots of land. To strengthen industry, it offered financial incentives to make factory workers labor harder, allowed some private ownership of businesses, and eliminated facilities that performed poorly. The nation also quit trying to make steel in backyards because it had been a failure.

Mao the All-Powerful

Even though Peng had been accurate in his assessment of the situation, he was punished for being truthful. He was dismissed as minister of defense and spent many years in forced labor camps. Mao was so powerful that it was dangerous to challenge him even when everyone knew he was wrong. His power stemmed not only from the positions he held but from the deep reverence most Chinese had for the leader of the Communist revolution.

Mao displayed this power during the meeting at Lushan. After accepting the blame for the failure of the Great Leap, he told the other Communist leaders that if his apology was not good enough he would "go to the countryside to lead the peasants to overthrow the government. If those of you in the Liberation Army won't follow me, then I will go and find a Red Army, and organize another Liberation Army."[36] The officials knew that Mao's threat was not an idle one. They backed down on criticizing him any further because they feared that Mao could lead another revolt that would topple their government.

Chapter Three

China Becomes a Military and Political Power

China was so weak for nearly a century before Mao Zedong led the Communists to power that foreign countries had repeatedly forced it to surrender territory and economic concessions. The foreign bullying began in the 1840s, when Great Britain seized Hong Kong, and continued through Japan's attempt during World War II to conquer the entire nation. The humiliation Chinese people felt over this weakness had led many of them to support the Communists, who promised to make China strong enough to stand up to other countries. On September 10, 1949, just ten days before Mao declared the birth of the People's Republic of China, he proudly proclaimed that China no longer had to fear foreign countries: "Ours will no longer be a nation subject to insult and humiliation. Our revolution has won the sympathy and acclaim of the people of all countries. We have friends all over the world. Our national defense will be consolidated and no [foreigners] will ever again be allowed to invade our land."[37]

Although Mao could not have dreamed it would happen so soon, within a year China would go to war to fulfill that vow.

China Becomes an Asian Power

World War II left Asian countries shattered and weak. Even Japan, which had dominated Asia for decades, was reduced to a shell of its former might. China had once been the most powerful nation in Asia, and historian Immanuel C.Y. Hsu writes that the PRC moved swiftly after the war to reclaim military and political supremacy over its neighbors: "[China's] relations with other Asian states reflected its intense drive for leadership in Asia."[38]

The People's Liberation Army was one of the world's most powerful

Communist troops construct a bridge and ferry troops across a Tibetan river during China's October 1950 invasion of Tibet.

armies, and China soon flexed that military might to reclaim a neighboring country it had once ruled. China had governed Tibet for several centuries until the Qing dynasty was overthrown in 1912. When Mao met with Joseph Stalin on January 22, 1950, he asked Stalin for help from the Soviet air force in transporting supplies for an invasion of Tibet. Stalin agreed, saying, "It's good that you are preparing to attack. The Tibetans need to be subdued."[39] Like Mao, Stalin believed it was proper to spread Communism to another country by force.

Forty thousand Chinese soldiers crossed into Tibet on October 7, 1950, and eas-

ily overwhelmed the nation's tiny army. China justified the invasion by claiming it was "liberating" Tibet from the control of Western nations such as Great Britain. Tibet, however, protested the takeover to the United Nations (UN) and said China was mistaken in saying it was liberating Tibet: "Liberation from whom and what? Ours was a happy country with a solvent [stable] government."[40] Neither the UN nor any other nation, however, came to the aid of Tibet, which became a Chinese province known as the Tibet Autonomous Region.

China was content to establish peaceful diplomatic relations with other Asian nations, such as India, Pakistan, and Burma, even though they were not Communist. However, China's attitude toward several other neighboring nations was shaped by its dedication to spreading Communism. When the PRC allied itself with the Soviet Union, Mao had claimed that "the Chinese must lean either to the side of imperialism or to the side of [Communism]. There can be no exception."[41] This belief led China to play a role in the only two military clashes of the Cold War—the Korean War and the Vietnam War.

The Cold War Turns Hot

The Cold War was the political, economic, and military struggle during the second half of the twentieth century between Communist countries and democratic nations such as the United States. This conflict began at the end of World War II in 1945, when the Soviet Union claimed territory it had won in battle against Germany and Japan. In Europe, the Soviets used military force to make part of defeated Germany and several other countries adopt Communism. In Asia, the Soviets backed the Chinese Communist Party's civil war and supported Communist movements in Korea and French Indochina, the colony France established in the nineteenth century by combining Vietnam, Cambodia, and Laos.

Korea exists on a peninsula that dangles downward from China's northeastern coast. China and Korea had been peaceful neighbors for many centuries, but Japan had ruled Korea since 1910. When Japan surrendered in August 1945, Soviet and U.S. soldiers both occupied about half of Korea. After both sides refused to give up areas they controlled, they agreed to divide the nation into North and South Korea along the thiry-eighth parallel.

For the next five years, the two Koreas existed peacefully but tensely. But when China defeated the Guomindang, North Korean dictator Kim Il Sung decided he wanted all of Korea to become Communist. On January 19, 1950, Kim asked Stalin for permission to invade South Korea. Stalin approved but told Kim that he "must rely on Mao, who understands Asian affairs beautifully"[42] for any help in conducting the war. Six months later, on June 25, the North Korean People's Army (NKPA) invaded South Korea to begin the Korean War.

China Enters the War

North Korea's devastating surprise attack enabled it to defeat South Korean soldiers and their U.S. military advisers and take control of most of South Korea. In September, however, a UN force composed of soldiers from the United States and other countries landed in South Korea and pushed the invaders back above the thirty-eighth parallel. Commanding general Douglas MacArthur was so emboldened by victory that he pursued the North Koreans into their homeland. The UN force crossed into North Korea on October 1, and by October 7 it had captured the North Korean capital of Pyongyang.

MacArthur invaded North Korea despite a warning that China had issued.

In a comment aimed at the United States on October 1, premier Zhou Enlai stated that China "will not tolerate foreign aggression and will not stand aside should the imperialists wantonly invade the territory of their neighbor [North Korea]."[43] MacArthur ignored an even stronger threat Zhou made on October 4 when he declared, "The South Koreans did not matter, but American intruders into North Korea would encounter Chinese resistance."[44]

Faced with the threat of North Korea's defeat, Mao called a special meeting of top CCP officials to discuss what to do. Several leaders argued it would be disastrous for China to fight because it was still trying to recover from years of its own civil war. But Mao wanted to help North Korea. After admitting that arguments against fighting were strong ones, Mao said, "When a neighbor is in mortal danger, it is hard just to stand by and watch, no matter how logical such a course may be."[45] Mao, however, was not concerned only with helping a neighbor. He felt China had no choice but to fight because he believed the UN force, which had pulled within 100 miles (161km) of China's bor-

General Douglas Macarthur, seated, sorely underestimated Chinese reaction to the fall of North Korea. He invaded North Korea in October 1950.

der, would continue on and invade China after it subdued North Korea.

Mao's arguments were so persuasive that, on October 5, the committee decided to fight the advancing UN troops. In an order Mao issued asking for volunteers to fight in Korea, he told them:

> In order to support the Korean people's war of liberation and to resist the attacks of U.S. imperialism and its running dogs, thereby safeguarding the interests of the people of Korea, China and all the other countries in the East, I herewith order the Chinese People's Volunteers to march speedily to Korea and join the Korean comrades in fighting the aggressors and winning a glorious victory.[46]

China Becomes a World Power

Two weeks later three hundred thousand Chinese soldiers entered North Korea and began fighting isolated battles against UN and South Korean soldiers. In late November Mao orchestrated the first major Chinese attack after MacArthur had foolishly split his forces, sending one group up the eastern side of North Korea and the other up the western coast in a final push to defeat the North Koreans. Mao infiltrated his troops between the two advancing columns of soldiers and attacked on November 25. The maneuver caught the invading troops by surprise, and in a few weeks the Chinese made them retreat into South Korea.

Mao was ecstatic at the success Chinese soldiers had over an army consisting mainly of U.S. soldiers, who were considered invincible after having won World War II. Mao claimed proudly and belligerently that China was now strong enough to stand up to any country: "We have won a great victory. We have taken the measure of the U.S. armed forces. The Chinese people are now organized, they are not to be trifled with. Once they are provoked to anger, things can get very tough."[47]

China's entry into the conflict evened the strength of the opposing forces and produced a stalemated war that neither side could win. Although the fighting continued until July 27, 1953, when a cease-fire went into effect, neither side made any major territorial gains. The war ended with both North and South Korea occupying the same areas they had held before the conflict began.

China gained immense prestige from having battled the United States to a draw. Military historian David Rees claims that "China's intervention in Korea and its initial victories over MacArthur's forces made the new China a world power."[48] Rees also claims the war increased Mao's personal stature so greatly that he became the political equal of Soviet leaders who succeeded Stalin after Stalin died in early 1953. However, the new respect for China and Mao came at a terrible cost. In addition to spending hundreds of millions of dollars to fight the war, an estimated nine hundred thousand Chinese soldiers were wounded or

The Korean War and China

The People's Republic of China gained great prestige by fighting the United States and United Nations to a draw in the Korean War. In The Search for Modern China, *author Jonathan D. Spence explains that this success came at a great price:*

The Chinese never released exact figures since they claimed that all their troops in [the Korean War] were "volunteers," not regular army personnel. But the staggering losses of close to one million men, many of whom were killed in the last year of the war by the overwhelming fire power of the UN forces, gave Chinese military leaders pause. . . . The domestic significance of the war was profound. Uppermost was the suffering of hundreds of thousands of Chinese troops, who fought in harsh winter weather with inadequate clothing, insufficient food, and little ammunition, against an enemy with overwhelming superiority in air and artillery power. The courageous but costly charges that the Chinese mounted against well-entrenched enemy emplacements amazed the foreign troops who witnessed them. This very courage gave rise to a new mystique of Chinese endurance and heroism, which was elaborated in the People's Republic by an outpouring of literature, films, plays, and tales of model soldier-heroes that reinforced the values of sacrifice and revolution.

Jonathan D. Spence, *The Search for Modern China.* New York: Norton, 1990, p. 531.

killed. Among the slain was Mao Anying, one of Mao's two sons.

The huge expenditure of money and manpower to help a Communist neighbor was one reason that China was reluctant a few years later to play a major role in the Vietnam War.

China Helps Another Communist Neighbor

While China was winning its civil war in the late 1940s, Communists in neighboring Vietnam were also fighting for control of their country. The situation in Vietnam was different than in China because France ruled Vietnam as part of a colony called Indochina. Led by Ho Chi Minh, the Vietnamese were trying to force the French to leave so that they could govern themselves. In early 1950 China was the first country to recognize the Democratic Republic of Vietnam, the Communist nation that Ho was trying to establish. China also gave Ho weapons and other supplies to continue Vietnam's fight for independence.

In May 1954 France surrendered to end the war following a stunning defeat at Dien Bien Phu. Both sides then agreed to meet in Geneva, Switzerland, to work out a peace settlement. Representatives of several other countries joined the talks, including Zhou, the Chinese premier. Zhou helped the Vietnamese negotiate the Geneva Accords, which allowed the nation to be split into North and South Vietnam as Korea had been a decade earlier. The Vietnamese Communists had not wanted the nation to be partitioned, but Zhou persuaded them to quit haggling over the issue. "After French withdrawal, the whole of Vietnam will be yours [for the taking],"[49] Zhou told them.

He believed it was in Vietnam's best interests to end the war and begin building a Communist nation.

The two Vietnams were supposed to reunite in 1956 and have an election that included voters in both countries. When South Vietnam refused to take part because it feared the Communists would win, the North Vietnamese began a civil war to take control of all Vietnam. The conflict escalated into a major war in the early 1960s, when the United States sent hundreds of thousands of soldiers to help defend the South Vietnamese.

The entry of U.S. troops made some PRC leaders believe Chinese soldiers

Mao Zedong meets with Ho Chi Minh in Beijing in 1955. Mao was the first to recognize the North Vietnam government.

Why Mao Zedong Helped Vietnam

Historian Qiang Zhai claims that Mao Zedong helped Vietnamese Communists defeat France because of his desire to spread Communism throughout the world.

The sense of an international mission to support [Communist] revolution in Asia [convinced Mao Zedong to] lend a hand to Ho Chi Minh. When Mao committed himself to revolution, he was determined to transform not only China but also the world. [Mao] and his comrades perceived a close connection between the Chinese and world revolutions. An international revolution would help consolidate and legitimize the Chinese revolution. An internal party directive on March 14, 1950, exemplified the CCP's [Chinese Communist Party's] conception of the linkage between the Chinese and world revolutions. "After the victory of our revolution," the document declared, "to assist in every possible way the Communist parties and people in all oppressed nations in Asia to win their liberation is an international obligation that the CCP and the Chinese people cannot shirk. It is also one of the most important methods to consolidate the victory of the Chinese revolution in the international arena."

Qiang Zhai, *China and the Vietnam Wars, 1950–1975*. Chapel Hill: University of North Carolina Press, 2000, pp. 20–21.

should fight as they had in Korea. Mao did not agree with them. In July 1966 Mao publicly declared that "revolution or people's war in any country is the business of the masses in that country."[50] Historians believe Mao shied away from a total commitment in the Vietnam War because he believed the Chinese needed to concentrate their resources on their own nation, which was still trying to recover from the Great Leap's flawed economic policies. The North Vietnamese then turned to the Soviets for help in the conflict.

North Vietnam eventually forced the United States to quit fighting and won control of the entire country. In a book on China's involvement in the Vietnam War, historian Qiang Zhai claims that, like the United States, "China also failed in Vietnam."[51] He believes China failed because it forced the Vietnamese into a stronger alliance with the Soviets, thus giving the Soviets a stronger presence in Asia. That was bad for China because it had become a bitter rival with the Soviet Union for supremacy as the world's most powerful Communist nation.

China's failure regarding Vietnam was minor compared to its inability to master its relations with another nation.

That was the Republic of China which Chiang Kai-shek and the Guomindang had established on Taiwan.

Failure to Take Taiwan

After Chiang and his supporters fled to Taiwan in 1949, it was generally assumed that the PRC would soon defeat them and reclaim the small island, which lies only 100 miles (161km) from the Chinese coast. The reason for that belief was that the United States was no longer willing to help the Guomindang after it had lost the civil war. On January 5, 1950, U.S. president Harry Truman stated, "The United States will not pursue a course which will lead to involvement in civil conflict in China."[52] Truman's position, however, changed overnight when China entered the Korean War. He began supplying the ROC with weapons and ordered the U.S. Navy to patrol the strait between Taiwan and China so that the PRC could not invade Taiwan.

President Dwight D. Eisenhower continued to protect Taiwan after he was elected in 1952. In September 1954 the PRC began a massive artillery bombardment of Jinmen, another island near Taiwan. Eisenhower threatened

In September 1954 President Eisenhower ordered the U.S. Navy to patrol the waters off Taiwan in response to the Chinese government's artillery bombardment of the island of Jinmen.

China with military action, including nuclear bombs, if it did not stop the attack. After the bombardment had continued for several more months, U.S. officials issued an even stronger warning to China in March 1955. A week later Zhou responded that "the Chinese people do not want to have war with the U.S.A. The Chinese government is willing to sit down and enter into negotiations with the U.S. government."[53] The two sides held talks, and on May 1 China ceased its eight-month bombardment. Chinese officials had realized that Taiwan was not worth risking war with the United States, which could have destroyed huge parts of China with atomic weapons.

Taiwan is still known by many people as Formosa, the Portuguese word for "beautiful," which was what early Portuguese explorers had named the island. By either name, the island remained a bitter reminder to the PRC of its failure to achieve a complete victory over the Guomindang. The leaders of the small island, which is only 240 miles (386km) long and 98 miles (158km) wide, continued to maintain that it still had the right to rule China. Even worse for the PRC was that the UN continued to allow Taiwan to hold the seat reserved for China. The UN did that because the PRC was considered an international outcast for using force to conquer Tibet and for opposing UN forces in the Korean War.

Mao Zedong and Atomic Weapons

Many people around the world were frightened when the People's Republic of China exploded its first nuclear bomb on October 16, 1964, because of comments Mao had made about nuclear war. In November 1957 Mao claimed at the Conference of World Communist Parties in Moscow that Communist China had so many people that it could survive an atomic war. Mao even claimed that a war that killed hundreds of millions of people might be a good thing because it could lead to a Communist takeover of the entire planet:

Let us speculate. If war broke out, how many people would die? There are 2.7 billion people in the entire world, and one-third of them may be lost. If the worst comes to the worst, perhaps one-half would die. But there would still be one-half left; imperialism [non-Communist countries] would be razed to the ground and the whole world would become socialist. After a number of years, the world's population would once again reach 2.7 billion and certainly become even bigger.

Quoted in Philip Short, *Mao: A Life*. New York: Henry Holt, 1999, p. 489.

Mao was furious over China's inability to conquer Taiwan. He was also angry that China had to back down against the United States because it did not have nuclear weapons of its own. That made Mao determined to add that powerful weapon to China's arsenal.

China Becomes a Nuclear Power

In the late 1950s the PRC began a program to develop a nuclear bomb. It is believed that China spent more than $4 billion in the next few years to develop such a weapon. This costly expenditure came at a time when millions of people were starving to death because of the disastrous economic policies of the Great Leap. The funds could have purchased food to feed hungry Chinese people, but Communist leaders believed it was more important that China join the United States and the Soviet Union as the world's only nuclear powers.

China exploded its first nuclear bomb on October 16, 1964, at Lop Nor in the Gobi Desert. Chinese people rejoiced that their nation had the technical knowledge to build such a powerful weapon, but no one was happier than Mao. China's powerful leader even composed a short poem to honor the event: "Atom bomb goes off when it is told, Ah, what boundless joy!"[54]

Chapter Four

China's Continuous Revolution

The revolution Mao Zedong brought to the Chinese people was not confined to Communist forms of government and economics. Mao also wanted to shape and control the beliefs Chinese people had about everything from religion to their families. In April 1958, while Mao was formulating the disastrous policies of the Great Leap Forward, he commented that the Chinese were ideal for his goal of fostering continuous revolution:

China's 600 million people have two remarkable peculiarities; they are, first of all, poor, and secondly blank. That may seem like a bad thing, but it is really a good thing. Poor people want change, want to do things, want revolution. A clean sheet of paper has no blotches, and so the newest and most beautiful words can be written on it, the newest and most beautiful pictures can be painted on it.[55]

Those words show Mao's arrogant confidence that he could manipulate the Chinese into believing anything. In the three decades Mao ruled China, he created several mass movements to control people's thoughts and actions. The most powerful was the Great Proletarian Cultural Revolution. Mao began this disastrous event in 1966, and the ill effects it caused for China did not end until he died on September 9, 1976. Mao, however, began shaping Chinese thought from the moment the People's Republic of China was born on October 1, 1949.

Changing People's Thoughts

When the Chinese Communist Party began ruling China, it forced everyone to learn Communist ideology; children were taught such ideas in school, and adults studied them at work. The PRC also organized people into large groups, such as the All-China Federation of Democratic Youth, which had 18 million members by 1953. The organizations helped educate people about Communism and made it easy for the government to mobilize crowds for political demonstrations, parades, and other events that showed public support for the government.

The Communists tried to make people give up traditional beliefs that might keep them from dedicating themselves completely to Communism. For example, they opposed religion because they did not want people to consider it more important than Communism. They also tried to change the way people thought about their families. In China, people had always considered family the most important thing in their lives. This belief was summed up in a

Members of the All China Federation of Democratic Youth lead children in a class in Beijing. The organization had 18 million members by 1953.

famous fable about a dutiful son who refused to turn his father over to officials after he had stolen a sheep. In 1951 newspaper stories made a hero of Li Kuohsin after his father, who owned a lot of land, had rebelled against Communist rule. When Li's father fled and could not be found, Li told officials where his father was hiding. Li explained why he betrayed his father: "I went to the police bureau and informed the responsible comrade [Communist official]. Then I went to my father and demanded that he recant his past and reform. He said, 'How could you do this to me?' [After his father was arrested Li said] I felt light-hearted. I was happy, for I had rid the people of a dangerous character."[56]

Stories about how Li was more loyal to the state than his family was one way in which the Communists tried to mold beliefs people had. The government did this by controlling the news that people could read or hear. The state's control of the media helped the PRC conduct its Resist-America/Aid-Korea propaganda campaign during the Korean War. The Communists blamed the conflict on the United States and United Nations and not North Korea, which had started the conflict. The effort made Chinese people hate Western countries so much that they did not oppose Communist leaders

A Family Is Separated

Yafei Hu explains how her parents were sent to the countryside during the Cultural Revolution because they were intellectuals:

My parents were sent to the province of Shandong, about three hundred miles from Beijing. My mother worked in a wheat field; my father was in charge of a chicken farm. Children were not allowed to go with their parents, so my brother and sister and I lived in an adolescent center in Beijing. We got to visit our parents once a year during the Spring Festival, which is the Chinese New Year. We wrote to our parents, and they wrote to us. Every time my mother wrote, we could see the tears on the paper. Sometimes she made us laugh, too, at the thought of our father being a chicken farmer. He didn't know anything at all about chickens! There were a lot of laughter and a lot of tears. After one year, my brother was sent to an army farm in Inner Mongolia. He was sixteen. My mother was heartbroken, because Inner Mongolia is a desolate place with a harsh climate.

Quoted in Elizabeth Lutyens, "Red Guard in Monument Square," *Independent School*, Fall 1991, p. 37.

when they expelled all foreign business-people, educators, and religious missionaries. The Communists did that to keep the Chinese people from hearing any facts or viewpoints that conflicted with those their leaders disseminated.

Let a Hundred Flowers Bloom

The Communists also tried to control writers, actors, educators, artists, and others who were considered intellectuals. The PRC punished intellectuals who criticized the government by imprisoning them or sending them to work in factories or on farms while being reeducated in Communist principles. Such actions were restrained during the first few years of the PRC's existence, however, because officials believed they needed this educated elite to help the young nation grow.

In 1957 Mao began a campaign to win the full support of intellectuals by allowing them more freedom to express themselves and even to criticize the party. In a speech on February 27, 1957, Mao said, "Letting a hundred flowers blossom and a hundred schools of thought contend is the policy for promoting the progress of the arts and the sciences and a flourishing [Communist] culture in our land."[57] Mao even encouraged other officials to "listen to opinions, especially unpleasant ones. Let people speak up. The sky will not fall. Don't think you are always right."[58]

Students at Peking University created a "Democratic Wall" on which they placed posters and articles criticizing Communism and pointing out mistakes that government officials had made. They spoke out against government censorship and questioned whether the state should have so much power over individuals. Huang Qiun explained why he and other intellectuals felt driven to point out such problems: "If a writer does not have the courage to reveal the dark diseases of society, does not have the courage to participate positively in solving the crucial problems of people's lives, and does not have the courage to attack all the deformed, sick, black things, then can he be called a writer?"[59]

Even though Mao had invited the criticism, it infuriated him. On May 25 he angrily told delegates to the Youth League Congress that "all words and actions that deviate from [Communism] are completely mistaken."[60] In June the PRC began punishing people for attacking Communist ideas and officials. A few people were executed, and as many as seven hundred thousand were sentenced to "reform through labor" on farms and in factories. In between their work shifts, they had to attend classes for Communist reeducation. This punishment lasted for several years, and many were never allowed to return to their former homes and jobs.

Some historians believe Mao used the "hundred flowers" campaign to expose and punish critics while others believe he had mistakenly believed he could win their support. There is no disagreement, however, on why Mao ignited the Great Proletarian Cultural

Revolution in 1966—it was his response to the aftermath of the failure of the Great Leap Forward.

Political Power and More Revolution

After Mao accepted partial blame for the Great Leap's disastrous economic and social consequences, he surrendered some of his political power to more moderate leaders like Liu Shaoqi, Zhou Enlai, and Deng Xiaoping so they could retool the ailing economy. But as the years passed, Mao became jealous of the power others now wielded. He also began to fear that China was losing its revolutionary commitment to Communism. It especially angered Mao that they ignored suggestions he made, such as resurrecting huge farm communes, which he believed were needed to preserve the purity of Chinese Communism.

Mao bolstered his political power by aligning himself with Lin Biao, whom he had made defense minister in 1959 after punishing Peng Dehuai for criticizing the Great Leap. Lin had won Mao's favor by encouraging people to worship Mao as China's greatest leader. He collected Mao's speeches and writings on various subjects in *Quotations from Chairman Mao Tse-tung*, which became known as "the Little Red Book" because of its red cover. He ordered soldiers to study the book, and in the 1960s everyone in China read it. Lin claimed dramatically that "once Mao Tse-tung's thought is grasped by the broad masses, it becomes an inexhaust-

Lin Biao, right, was Mao's right hand-man and was instrumental in perpetuating Mao as China's greatest leader.

ible source of strength and a spiritual atom bomb of infinite power."[61]

As Mao's popularity grew, he began plotting to regain control of China from party leaders who he believed were straying from Communist principles. He said this threat came from "people in authority *within the party* who are taking the capitalist road."[62] One of them was Liu, who had allowed peasants to own land again. But Mao also feared that intellectuals were trying to erode support for Communism through plays, movies, and written articles. For example, he claimed that a play called *The Dismissal of Hai Rui from Office* was a veiled attack on himself.

Mao's wife, Chiang Qing, was a former actress. He enlisted her and Chen Boda, Kang Sheng, and Wang Dongxin —minor Communist officials who were Chiang 's friends—to help him battle people he believed were using popular culture to undermine Communism. Chiang and the others formed the Cultural Revolution Committee to monitor the work of artists. The committee's attacks on playwrights and film directors helped stir up anger against party officials and intellectuals. Although the committee gave the Great Proletarian Cultural Revolution its name, it was Mao who unleashed the revolution in his attempt to regain power.

On May 16, 1966, Mao openly criticized Liu and Deng, who he claimed were setting China on a road that would lead it back to a capitalist economy. He appealed to young people to rise up against these "capitalist roaders" and

return to his vision of Communism. "Liberate the little ones!" Mao said. "I shall call for rebellion in the provinces. They will rise up and tear down the palace of the King of Hell."[63] The "King of Hell" was Mao's dramatic nickname for Liu.

The Cultural Revolution Begins

One of the first to heed Mao's call was Nie Yuanzi, a young philosophy teacher at Beijing University. On May 24 she and some friends put up a poster titled "Bombard the Headquarters!" that called for punishment of people who opposed Mao's ideas. Brightly colored posters were an accepted Chinese political tool to criticize people or ideas. When Mao ordered the poster and its message publicized throughout China on June 1, the news stories touched off a wave of similar protests.

Luan is a Chinese word that means "chaos" or "disturbance." Mao enjoyed creating such situations because he believed they forced individuals to accept revolutionary new ways to do things. *Luan* now reigned throughout China as young people began acting on Mao's desire to make everyone reject Chinese traditions and embrace Communist doctrine. Mao did this by ordering participants to destroy the "Four Olds," by which he meant old customs, old habits, old culture, and old thinking.

Mao closed all schools. Young people, most of them aged fifteen to twenty-five, formed Red Guard units dedicated to him. There were about 20 million Red Guards from 1966 to 1968. Most Red Guards were students, but workers, rural peasants, and former soldiers also joined the Cultural Revolution. Quinghua University Red Guards in Beijing claimed in a poster that their aim was to "turn the old world upside down, smash it to pieces, pulverize it, and create chaos—the greater the confusion the better!"[64] Red Guards physically destroyed books, works of art, and 4,922 historical heritage sites, including religious temples; some of the historical artifacts and sites were thousands of years old.

More disturbingly, Red Guards attacked people they believed opposed Mao or clung to old traditions. Victims of this violence included teachers, factory administrators, party members, and parents. The guards publicly humiliated these so-called enemies of the state, who they mockingly called ghosts and monsters. Guards dragged people out of their homes or offices, surrounding them and jeering at them. They sometimes forced them to parade through city streets wearing dunce caps and signs listing their alleged crimes; bystanders verbally taunted them and even threw rocks and bottles. In "struggle sessions" that could last for days, guards made people confess to alleged offenses, such as rejecting Communist ideals. People who did not confess were beaten and sometimes tortured until they did; some died from the physical abuse, and others were so humiliated and scared that they committed suicide.

The Red Guards revived Communist hatred of rich people like landlords, and they persecuted their descendants. Ji-Li Chiang remembers how her teachers and classmates rejected her after they learned her grandfather had been a landlord: "Heaven and earth switched places when I was 12 years old. [In] just a few months I went from being an outstanding student to being an outcast. Classmates and kids in my neighborhood bullied me and my siblings."[65]

In just a few weeks, violence and destruction engulfed China. When party officials complained to Mao in late August, he ignored their concerns and told them, "In my opinion, we should let the chaos go on for a few months."[66] The violence lasted much longer because other leaders were afraid to stop what Mao had set in motion.

The Violence Worsens

Mao loved the Cultural Revolution because he was idolized. In its first three months, 13 million Red Guards came to Beijing to cheer him in huge public rallies in Tiananmen Square. The guards were allowed to travel free by train and were provided food and housing wherever they went to hunt down Mao's enemies and spread his revolutionary ideas. The Red Guards had such power because the CCP's Central Committee had formally passed a sixteen-point program on August 8, 1966, in which it gave its blessing to the movement. Written mainly by Mao, it endorsed the Cultural Revolution and advised everyone to "trust the masses, rely on

The Red Guards Worshipped Mao Zedong

On August 18, 1966, Beijing University teacher Nie Yuanzi spoke at a rally. Her words show how fanatically devoted the Red Guards were to Mao Zedong:

A Great Proletarian Cultural Revolution without parallel in history is being carried out in our country under the leadership of our great leader Chairman Mao. This is a revolution of world significance. We will smash the old world to smithereens, create a new world and carry the Great Proletarian Cultural Revolution through to the end. . . . Chairman Mao is the reddest sun in our hearts [and we] shall bear Chairman Mao's teachings firmly in mind. [We] face a mountain of swords and a sea of flames, but we also have a great beacon light—Mao thought which will surely guide us to victory. . . . This is the happiest and most important moment in our lives. We'll read his works, follow his teaching, act according to his instructions and be his good pupils for the rest of our lives.

Quoted in Asia Research Centre, *The Great Cultural Revolution in China*. Rutland, VT: C.E. Tuttle, 1968, p. 442.

Red Guards march with wooden rifles thru the streets of Beijing in support of Mao's Cultural Revolution in 1966.

them and respect their initiatives. Cast out fear. Do not be afraid of disturbances."[67]

The Cultural Revolution, however, gradually spiraled out of control as the guards persecuted hundreds of thousands of people, including many who had bravely fought to bring about the Communist revolution. By October 1966 the guards had even stripped Liu and Deng of their party positions and had imprisoned them. Tens of thousands of people, including Deng, were sent for reeducation. The violence worsened as the number of participants grew, but officials were afraid to stop it because they feared the guards would turn on them. Xie Fuzhi, who headed China's national police, said, "If people are beaten to death, it's none of our business."[68] The violence gradually swelled to include clashes between rival Red Guard units who fought pitched battles involving thousands of combatants.

The Red Guards eventually began fighting for control of entire cities. In January 1967 the Workers' Headquarters, a group made up of laborers, seized power in Shanghai from local Communist leaders and declared itself that city's rightful government. Mao persuaded the group to set up a Revolutionary Committee composed of workers, Communists, and People's Liberation Army officers to govern the city. For several years, this format

Students Kill a Teacher

Ken Ling, a sixteen-year-old Red Guard in Fujian, describes the beating death of a teacher:

Teacher Chen, over 60 years old, was dragged up to the second floor of a classroom building and beaten with fists and broomsticks. He passed out several times, but was brought back to consciousness with cold water being splashed on his face. He could hardly move his body; his feet were cut by glass and thorns. He shouted, "Why don't you kill me? Kill me!" This lasted for six hours, until he lost control of his excrement. They tried to force a stick into his rectum [to stop it]. He collapsed for the last time. They poured cold water on him again. It was too late. People began to run away [and] the killers were a little frightened. . . . After a night filled with dreadful nightmares, I mustered enough courage to go to school the next day to witness more of this torture. After 10 days or so, I became used to it; a blood-smeared body or a shriek no longer made me feel uneasy.

Quoted in Philip Short, *Mao: A Life*. New York: Henry Holt, 1999, p. 545.

of shared power between the three groups became an accepted way to govern many communities.

Mao Finally Acts

By the summer of 1967, China was on the verge of civil war because of continued fighting and violence by Red Guard units and other radical groups. When Mao finally realized that the Cultural Revolution was endangering the authority of the CCP itself to rule China, he ordered the PLA to begin restoring order. The army used physical force to seize control of government again in some cities, but the chaos of the Cultural Revolution was so strong that some disorder continued for another year.

In July 1968 Mao decided it was finally time to end the rampage of the Red Guards that was causing so much domestic chaos. He summoned Beijing's five top Red Guard leaders, including Nie, to a meeting and reprimanded them for "the mad fratricidal combats"[69] they were engaging in. He also ordered Red Guard units to disband. When a militant unit at Beijing's Quinghua University refused, Mao sent forty thousand workers and soldiers to physically remove them on July 27.

Even though most of the Red Guards heeded Mao's orders to disband, Mao realized he needed to do something to stop them from starting another revolution. On December 22, 1968, the *People's Daily* newspaper in Beijing published an order from Mao that read, "School graduates will be going to the countryside to get re-educated by the peasants."[70] The real reason for what was dubbed the "Down to the Countryside Movement" was to eliminate any future threat from the Red Guards. Between 1968 and 1972, as many as 20 million Red Guards, along with other young people, were sent to rural areas. Many of them were never allowed to return to their homes to resume their old lives.

Mao had ordered the Red Guards to begin the Cultural Revolution. But he would later boast, "I am the black hand that suppressed the Red Guards."[71]

Mao Wins the Cultural Revolution

Although Mao's suppression of the Red Guards ended the violence and massive social disorder of the Cultural Revolution, the effects of the cultural storm Mao unleashed continued to affect China for nearly a decade. That was because the only winner in the Cultural Revolution was Mao, who used the chaos it created to regain leadership of China. At the Ninth Party Congress in April 1969, Mao was unanimously reelected chairman of the CCP as well as the party's powerful Central Committee. Mao used his power to influence China until his death in 1976. He restored revolutionary fervor in the Chinese people, eliminated thousands of Communist leaders who did not support him, and kept China from straying from the Communist ideal he had created for it.

Chapter Five

The Stuggle for Power Continues

On July 16, 1966, Mao Zedong swam and floated 9 miles (14km) down the Yangtze River near Wuhan. Mao's athletic feat on the eve of the Great Proletarian Cultural Revolution was designed to show that the seventy-two-year-old was strong enough physically to once again lead China. Mao liked to swim outdoors. When he did, aides often accompanied Mao to protect him. If they had trouble swimming, Mao would give them this advice: "Maybe you're afraid of sinking. Don't think about it. If you don't think about it, you won't sink. If you do, you will."[72]

Mao's legendary ability to stay afloat while others struggled has often been compared to his talent to remain above his rivals in China's continuing battles for political power. Mao had used this ability to regain control of the People's Republic of China during the Cultural Revolution's chaotic start. He would need the ability again in the revolution's final years as he faced two new battles for power. One struggle pitted Mao against Lin Biao, his chosen successor, and the other was between two factions of Communists with differing visions for China's future.

Mao Versus Lin

One reason for the continuing power struggle was that Mao never liked sharing power. In 1959, after Mao had allowed Liu Shaoqi to become China's president, he started the Cultural Revolution to get rid of Liu. And after naming Lin Biao his successor in April 1969, Mao grew as jealous of his protégé's new stature as he had of Liu's position. Mao also began to fear that the People's Liberation Army, which Lin commanded as defense minister, was becoming powerful enough to overthrow Mao. Ironically, Mao was to blame for the PLA's increased strength.

He was so grateful for PLA help in curbing Red Guard excesses that he rewarded army officials with eleven of twenty-one seats in the Politburo, which made key decisions in governing China. Mao did this despite his long-standing belief that "the [Communist] party commands the gun [army] and the gun will never be allowed to command the party."[73]

Mao also disagreed with Lin on several key policy issues. Their most serious difference was over China's relationship with the Soviet Union. In 1967 Mao had said that China needed to continually assess threats to its future: "Who are our enemies? Who are our friends? This is a question of the first importance for the revolution and it is likewise a question of the first importance for the great cultural revolution."[74] In the late 1960s Mao used this questioning attitude to change his mind about the Soviet Union and the United States.

There had been a growing political rift between China and the Soviet Union since the Great Leap Forward, when Mao ejected Soviet technical experts after they criticized his economic plans. Tension between them also increased in the mid-1960s, when Mao refused to send soldiers to fight in the Vietnam War. The growing hostility sometimes erupted in military clashes along the border the nations shared. On

Lin Biao was the leader of a plot to overthrow Mao in 1971. He would die under suspicious circumstances when he attempted to flee to the Soviet Union.

March 2, 1969, Chinese soldiers attacked Soviet forces on Chenbao Island on the Ussuri River as part of a continuing dispute over which country owned the island. The raid ignited a series of deadly clashes that pushed the Communist nations to the brink of war.

After the incident was resolved, Lin favored renewing China's friendship with the Soviets. But Mao believed instead that China should become friendlier with the United States, even though he had always demonized it as the world's richest capitalist nation. The Soviet Union was the main Cold War enemy of the United States. Mao believed the United States would welcome the chance to become an ally of the Chinese against the Soviets because it would unite two powerful nations against the USSR.

As the two leaders became estranged, Lin began to fear for his life. Lin knew that Mao had killed other rivals, and he privately told his friends, "Once he thinks someone is his enemy, he won't stop until the victim is put to death."[75] In 1971 Lin decided to kill Mao before Mao killed him.

The Plot to Kill Mao

Mao's hostility to Lin was apparent to everyone on May 1, 1971, when they stood together to review a parade celebrating Communism. Mao had already weakened Lin by firing several PLA commanders who backed him in political matters. Mao also moved the army unit considered most loyal to Lin away from Beijing so the PLA leader could not use the soldiers loyal to him to attack Mao. During the parade, Lin began sweating profusely because he was nervous standing next to someone he knew wanted to destroy him. Lin was so ill at ease that Mao ridiculed him for being nervous.

In August Mao tried to win the support of PLA commanders against Lin by visiting military bases in south and central China. Fearing that Mao would act against him if he succeeded, in early September Lin met with his son Lin Liguo, an air force general, and key aides to plan Mao's assassination. The conspirators considered several ways to murder Mao, from poison to staging a fatal car accident. In a document that later became public, they claimed, "If B-52 falls into our hands, the enemy battleships [senior leaders] will also be in our hands."[76] They named Mao "B-52" after the giant bombers the United States was using in the Vietnam War; the nickname was an admission of how powerful and dangerous their target was. They finally decided to kill Mao by bombing his train on September 8 while he traveled from Hangchow to Shanghai.

Premier Zhou Enlai discovered the assassination attempt and alerted Mao. He altered his travel plans to avoid the attack and arrived in Beijing unharmed on September 12. When Lin learned that Mao knew about the plot, he commandeered a military jet to escape to the Soviet Union; Lin would be welcome there because Soviet leaders hated Mao. On September 13 the plane

Leadership Changes Confused People

Historian Jonathan D. Spence explains how the constant leadership changes during the Cultural Revolution confused average people:

In an address [on] April 1, 1969, Lin [Biao said] China's former head of state Liu Shaoqi had "betrayed the Party [and] become a hidden traitor." In 1972 Premier Zhou Enlai announced that it was Lin Biao who had been the "renegade and traitor." Not surprisingly Chen villagers were as puzzled as anyone. "I had felt faithful to Mao," said one Chen Village peasant, recalling this period in [an interview], "but that Lin Biao stuff affected my thinking." Or as one of the urban youths assigned to the village [in 1971] put it: "When Liu Shaoqi was dragged down we'd been very supportive. But the Lin Biao affair provided us with a major lesson. We came to see that the leaders up there could say today that something is round; tomorrow that it's flat. We lost faith in the system." The credulity of the Chinese people had been stretched beyond all possible boundaries as leader after leader had first been praised to the skies and then vilified.

Jonathan D. Spence, *The Search for Modern China*. New York: Norton, 1990, p. 617.

took off at 12:32 A.M. from Beidahe, a seashore resort east of Beijing. Only ninety minutes after takeoff, however, everyone aboard was killed when the aircraft crashed in Outer Mongolia. Although Chinese officials reported that the plane crashed because it ran out of fuel, so few details about the incident are known that no one is sure what really happened.

Mao Accepts New Leadership

Mao had survived yet another battle for political supremacy, and once again he had to select new leaders to help him run China. One mistake Mao did not make twice was to give too much power to the military. He reduced the number of PLA officials in high party positions and warned army officers to "pay attention to military affairs."[77] Mao also decided that China needed more moderate leaders to restore stability to China after the Cultural Revolution's early chaos. He also wanted the moderates to serve as a counterweight to the power still wielded by his wife, Chiang Qing, and other radicals who had helped him start the disastrous revolution.

Mao began to rely on premier Zhou Enlai, a moderate who had stayed in power because everyone respected him. Zhou convinced Mao that the excesses of the Cultural Revolution had ousted many competent party officials who were not guilty of any crimes. Mao and Zhou brought back several hundred former officials to help run the country, including Deng Xiaoping, who had been secretary-general of the Chinese Communist Party from 1956 to 1967.

A moderate like Zhou, Deng had always relied on common sense over Communist ideology to govern. This attitude was summed up by his favorite classic Chinese proverb: "It doesn't matter if the cat is black or white, as long as it catches mice."[78] Deng had used this pragmatic approach to make changes to fix the Great Leap Forward's disastrous economic policies, such as downsizing the giant communes. But Deng's lack of dedication to Communist ideals led Red Guards to brand him an enemy of the state in 1966. Deng was stripped of his political posts and was exiled to rural Jianxi Province, where he survived by planting vegetables and raising chickens.

Zhou brought Deng back to Beijing in February 1973. Within a year Deng was helping run China as the nation's executive vice premier; he was later named a Politburo member and the PLA chief of staff. Deng downsized the PLA to make it a smaller threat to civilian rule. He and Zhou also created the Four Modernizations program to strengthen China's economy. Zhou presented the plan at a national party meeting in January 1975; it called for sweeping improvements to modernize the economy. In a speech several months later, Deng explained the plan:

> The first stage is to build an independent and relatively comprehensive industrial and economic system by 1980. The second will be to turn China into a powerful socialist country with modern agriculture, industry, national defense, and science and technology by the end of this century. The entire party and nation must strive for the attainment of this great objective.[79]

Zhou and Deng also began to work to end China's isolation from other nations, which had deepened during the Cultural Revolution's years of chaos. With Mao's consent, the first step in this effort was to reestablish diplomatic ties with the United States.

China Reenters the World

In December 1970 Zhou secretly contacted the United States about reestablishing diplomatic ties. The two nations exchanged diplomatic messages, and in July 1971 U.S. secretary of state Henry Kissinger secretly visited Beijing. Zhou and Kissinger worked out details for a visit by President Richard M. Nixon the following year. Nixon was a staunch anti-Communist. But like Mao, he believed an alliance of the two nations could prove beneficial in dealing with the Soviet Union.

When Nixon shook hands with Zhou after he landed in Beijing on February 27, 1972, Zhou told him, "Your handshake

Zhou Enlai's Speech

On February 27, 1972, Zhou Enlai, the premier of the People's Republic of China, made the following remarks at a banquet in Beijing honoring U.S. president Richard M. Nixon:

[This is] an event unprecedented in the history of the relations between China and the United States. The American people are a great people. The Chinese people are a great people. The peoples of our two countries have always been friendly to each other. But owing to reasons known to all, contacts between the two peoples were suspended for over 20 years. Now, through the common efforts of China and the United States, the gate to friendly contacts has finally been opened. At the present time it has become a strong desire of the Chinese and American peoples to promote the normalization of relations between the two countries and work for the relaxation of tension. We are confident that the day will surely come when this common desire of our two peoples will be realized.

Quoted in Richard M. Nixon, *Public Papers of the Presidents of the United States: Richard Nixon, 1972.* Washington, DC: Government Printing Office, 1972, p. 369.

When Zhou Enlai met with U.S. president Richard M. Nixon on February 27, 1972, it ended twenty-five years of noncommunication between the two powers.

came over the vastest ocean in the world—twenty-five years of no communication."[80] The handshake symbolized the historic new relationship between the two nations. The handshake was especially significant because in 1954 U.S. secretary of state John Foster Dulles had refused to shake hands with Zhou at the Geneva Conference on Vietnam.

Nixon met Mao that afternoon. When Nixon told Mao his writings had "changed the world," Mao humbly claimed, "I have not been able to change it. I have only been able to change a few places in the vicinity of Beijing."[81] At a banquet that night, Nixon declared, "There is no reason for us to be enemies. Neither of us seeks domination of the other. Neither of us wants to dominate the other."[82] The new, friendly relationship Nixon described was formalized in the Shanghai Communiqué, which both nations signed on February 28 in Shanghai. The document ended a major dispute between the nations over Taiwan. The government in Taiwan still claimed it was China's rightful ruler. The United States stated that "the Government of the People's Republic of China is the sole legal government of China [and] Taiwan is a province of China; the liberation of Taiwan is China's internal affair in which no other country has the right to interfere."[83]

The statement on Taiwan was not the only concession the United States gave up to secure improved relations with China. After the countries agreed to the trip in July 1971, U.S. officials dropped their opposition to the PRC's entry into the United Nations. Taiwan, with U.S. backing, had continued to represent China in the UN after 1949. But on October 25, 1971, UN delegates, with no U.S. opposition, voted to take China's seat away from Taiwan and give it to the PRC. The acceptance by the world organization and Nixon's visit helped China begin to establish diplomatic ties with other nations, which Zhou and Deng both wanted. They believed China needed to interact with other nations to strengthen its economy through trade and the acquisition of new technology. China even became friendly with Japan, for centuries a rival for supremacy in Asia and a nation that had invaded it during World War II.

The End of the Mao Era

Mao's meeting with Nixon helped China emerge from its international isolation. It was one of Mao's last personal triumphs because he was suffering from several illnesses. When Nixon greeted Mao, he told him, "You look very good," only to have Mao respond, "Appearances are deceiving."[84] Mao was already ill with Parkinson's disease, a weak heart, respiratory problems due to his lifelong smoking habit, and the onset of blindness caused by cataracts. In the next few years, Mao grew weaker after suffering a stroke, which partially paralyzed him and made his speech difficult to understand.

With Mao weakened by illness, radicals led by Mao's wife, Chiang , stepped up their attacks on moderates like Zhou and Deng. The radicals believed China should remain true to Communist doctrine. In the past they had unsuccessfully tried to stop Zhou and Deng from introducing plans that seemed to depart from Communist ideals. Mao had grown weary of this interference and repeatedly told Chiang to quit trying to control the nation. In December 1974 he had warned her, "You'd better be careful, don't let yourselves become a small faction of four."[85] There were three other leaders in the clique Chiang headed—Wang Hongwen, Zhang Chungqiao, and Yao Wenyuan.

When Zhou died on January 8, 1976, from cancer, an illness he had battled for four years, the power struggle intensified. The moderate faction suffered a blow on February 7 when Mao named Hua Guofeng to replace Zhou as premier instead of Deng, who had been expected to get the job. It is believed Mao chose Hua, a political newcomer, because he

An aging Mao meets with Richard Nixon in February 1972. The meeting was instrumental in China's emerging from its isolation and becoming a U.S. trading partner.

did not want to anger either faction. However, in early April hundreds of thousands of people held a series of tributes to Zhou in Tiananmen Square. Angered at the show of support for Zhou, the radicals ordered an armed militia they controlled to violently disperse the crowd; they killed or wounded hundreds of people. Chiang blamed Deng for the disorder, and he was stripped of his political posts. Deng fled to Guangzhou in southern China because General Xu Shiyou, the region's military governor, had offered to protect him from the radicals.

When Mao chose Hua, he told him, "With you in charge, I am at ease."[86]

Mao knew he was dying and he believed his compromise choice could prevent a battle for power that could hurt China. Mao's health continued to fail, and on September 2, 1976, he had a massive heart attack. He died seven days later on September 9. Mao had once said, "Ten thousand years are too long: seize the day, seize the hour!"[87] Mao had always been impatient to accomplish things, but time had finally run out for the man most responsible for making China a Communist nation.

The Gang of Four

More than a week of state and unofficial functions to honor Mao was capped by

Madam Mao sits in court during the Gang of Four trials. In 1981 she and her compatriots were found guilty of antiparty activities and were sentenced to long prison terms.

China Condemns the Cultural Revolution

In June 1981 delegates to a national Chinese Communist Party gathering approved a thirty-five-thousand-word resolution condemning the Great Proletarian Cultural Revolution. The resolution also blamed Mao Zedong for starting the disastrous event:

Practice has shown that the "Great Cultural Revolution" did not in fact institute a revolution or social progress in any sense, nor could it possibly have done so. It was we and not the enemy who were thrown into disorder by it. Therefore, from beginning to end, it did not turn "great disorder under heaven" into "great order under heaven." History has shown that the "Great Cultural Revolution," initiated by a leader laboring under a misconception and capitalized on by counter-revolutionary cliques, led to domestic turmoil and brought catastrophe to the party, the state, and the whole people. Comrade Mao far from making a correct analysis of many problems confused right and wrong and the people with the enemy. Herein lies the tragedy.

Quoted in Immanuel C.Y. Hsu, *China Without Mao: The Search for a New Order*. New York: Oxford University Press, 1990, p. 148.

a public funeral in Tiananmen Square attended by a half million people. In a televised eulogy, Hua quoted from a speech Mao had made during the Cultural Revolution: "We want unity, not dissension. We want to be open and aboveboard, not scheming and intriguing."[88]

During the funeral Hua stood between Chiang and Wang. But only four weeks later, on October 6, he arrested Wang, Zhang, and Yao when they showed up for a Politburo meeting. Hua read a statement that claimed, "You have entered into an anti-Party and anti-socialist alliance in a vain attempt to usurp the leadership of the Party and to seize power."[89] Chiang was arrested one hour later at her home, and as many as thirty other people linked to the four were taken into custody throughout China.

Hua arrested "the Gang of Four"—the nickname for Chiang and her accomplices—because he had learned they were plotting to overthrow him. The next day, the Politburo released a long list of charges that accused them of countless crimes, including plotting to kill Mao and Hua, forging Mao's signature on documents, and lying about Deng and other officials. In 1981 the four were tried and convicted of antiparty activities. Chiang, the former actress, was defiant and unrepentant: "Fine. Go ahead! [You] can kill me. Still

I regret nothing. I was right. I dare you to sentence me to death in front of one million people in Tiananmen Square."[90] All four were sentenced to long prison sentences but eventually were released; Chiang committed suicide in 1991.

The End of the Cultural Revolution

Historians claim the Cultural Revolution ended in October 1976 with the arrest of Chiang and her supporters be- cause they had played such a leading role in starting and keeping it going. Their arrest, however, was made possible by the death the previous month of Mao, who had been most responsible for unleashing the Cultural Revolution. Five years later, in June 1981, the CCP condemned the Cultural Revolution for having "caused the most devastating setback and heavy losses to the party, the state, and the people in the history of the People's Republic."[91]

Chapter Six

Deng Xiaoping Leads China in a New Direction

The death of Mao Zedong on September 9, 1976, marked the beginning of a new era for the People's Republic of China, one that would bring its people more freedom and prosperity than ever before. For nearly three decades Mao had shaped China according to a Communist vision that rejected capitalism and what he believed was its biggest evil—the pursuit of individual wealth. In the early 1960s Mao wrote that education should encourage "hard work and bitter struggles" for the nation's common good and that "it cannot emphasize personal material interests, and lead people into the private pursuit of 'a wife, a dacha [vacation home], a car, and a TV set.'"[92]

The man who followed Mao as the PRC's most powerful leader turned sharply away from Mao's beliefs. He became famous as the Communist who said "to get rich is glorious."[93] And al-though not everyone in China would become gloriously rich, Deng Xiaoping is credited with lifting more people out of poverty than any leader of any nation in history.

The Return of Deng

Deng was a small man, only 4 feet (1.2m) and 11 inches (28cm) tall, but he had been an able army commander and was a tough opponent in China's never-ending battles for political power. After Deng was exiled for the second time during the Cultural Revolution, he decided to fight back from Guangzhou, where General Xu Shiyou was protecting him. Deng won support for a political comeback from high-ranking military officers, older party leaders who were his friends, and younger Communists who backed reform.

Shortly after the Gang of Four was arrested, Deng returned to Beijing as part of his bid to return to power. When thousands of people gathered in Ti-ananmen Square on January 8, 1977, the first anniversary of Zhou Enlai's death, posters appeared praising Deng. One said that the "revolutionary situation was great [and] everyone was in high spirits"[94] when Deng was an official; others claimed he had been unfairly blamed for the unrest after Zhou's death. Deng and his supporters were responsible for the show of support.

In July 1977 public and private pressure engineered by Deng and his supporters forced Hua Guofeng to reinstate Deng to the positions he had lost the previous April—vice premier, Polit-buro member, and head of the Military Affairs Commission. Hua, however, was still more powerful than Deng and considered himself the custodian of Mao's beliefs. He and Deng began to clash over China's economy and foreign policy.

As Deng helped more victims of the Cultural Revolution return to their government positions, they supported him and his power base grew. Gradually, Deng began to wield more power than Hua. In August 1980 Deng forced Hua to resign as premier and replaced him with Zhao Ziyang. Although Deng allowed supporters like Zhao to hold of-

Deng Xiaoping, left, is shown with Hu Yaobang, right, at a party rally in Beijing. In 1980 Deng would force Hu to resign as premier.

fices that ranked above his, Deng was always the most powerful Chinese leader from 1978 to 1997. His authority was so great that he was referred to as "paramount leader." Deng used that power to transform China.

"Time to Prosper"

When Deng returned to power, he started to implement the Four Modernizations, which had been set aside because of opposition by radical Communists. The Four Modernizations were designed to strengthen China's overall economy through improvements in agriculture, industry, national defense, and science. To achieve that goal, Deng ignored Communist ideology and incorporated several capitalist elements into the Chinese economy. He broke up collectives so farmers could own their own land, encouraged individuals to start private businesses, and allowed foreign countries to invest in China. Deng also created special economic zones to develop industries that would provide more jobs.

These changes were drastic. China had always condemned individuals who worked only to make money for themselves and had isolated itself from capitalist nations like the United States, which were the only ones wealthy enough to invest in China. In 1978 Deng introduced two principles that justified such actions: "practice is the sole criterion of truth" and "seek truth from facts."[95] The short sayings meant that it was more important to have economic programs that worked than to follow

Communist doctrine. "China is poor," Deng argued. "Poverty cannot demonstrate the superiority of socialism. It is time to prosper. China has been poor a thousand years."[96]

Deng's plans started to lift China out of poverty.

China's New Economy

From 1979 to 1989 China's gross national product, the value of goods and services a nation produces, increased 9.2 percent annually. The substantial growth in China's overall economy was due to development of new industries, private businesses, an increase in agricultural production, and a boost in tourism as foreigners by the hundreds of thousands began visiting a nation that had long been closed to them. This economic growth translated into higher wages, especially in rural areas where 80 percent of China's population lived.

The average annual income in 1972 in Liu Lin village in Shaanxi Province was about 120 yuan in Chinese currency or about $60; by 1980 it had risen to 300 yuan ($150), and by 1987 to 450 yuan ($225). One factor in this rural income growth was higher rates farmers received for the portion of crops they had to sell the government even though they owned their own land. However, observers believe the biggest factor in farmer income growth was that people worked harder because they could keep any profit they made from their land. Yang Chiangli, a farmer in Fengyang County, explains how people responded to the profit incentive:

Deng Xiaoping Explains His Reforms

In 1984, Deng Xiaoping explained his economic reforms to a group of Japanese officials who visited China:

Proceeding from the realities in China, we must first of all solve the problem of the countryside. Eighty per cent of the population lives in rural areas, and China's stability depends on the stability of those areas. No matter how successful our work is in the cities, it won't mean much without a stable base in the countryside. We therefore began by invigorating the economy and adopting an open policy there, so as to bring the initiative of 80 per cent of the population into full play. We adopted this policy at the end of 1978, and after a few years it has produced the desired results. Now the [People's Republic of China] has decided to shift the focus of reform from the countryside to the cities. The urban reform will include not only industry and commerce but science and technology, education and all other fields of endeavor as well. In short, we shall continue the reform at home and open [China] still wider to the outside world.

Deng Xiaoping, "Build Socialism with Chinese Characteristics," June 30, 1984. www.english.peopledaily. com.cn/dengxp/vol3/text/c1220.html.

In our cooperative days we used to work all day, every day, year-in and year-out, but we got almost nothing done—work a little, take a break, work a little more, take another beak. We felt harassed and we produced very little. What we were doing looked like work but in fact we were stalling around. Now we make every minute count. Our labors produce results. We earn a good living.[97]

Other rural residents also benefited from Deng's economic plan. Foreign companies that made everything from athletic shoes to television sets created new jobs when they built factories in rural areas, where land was cheap. As farmers and workers made more money, other people started businesses to provide them with products and services. In Yinfeng in Sichuan Province, Wu Wanwu and his three sons opened a noodle shop and several other businesses. By 1983 the family's income from these enterprises had made them rich by rural standards.

Urban areas also benefited from the special zones China started for economic development. The designation allowed investment by both China and foreign companies in those areas to create new jobs. The first four zones in 1979 included cities like Shenzhen and Xiamen. In 1984 this special status was extended to fourteen more cities, including Tianjin, Shanghai, and Guang- zhou, which were already major commercial and industrial centers. Several cities, such as Beijing and Shanghai, also benefited from expanding tourism.

Deng's economic system depended heavily on financial investment from foreign companies. This meant that China had to improve its diplomatic relations with other countries.

China Embraces the World

Despite President Richard M. Nixon's historic 1972 visit, the two nations had never established normal diplomatic relations because of their continuing dispute over Taiwan. The United States had admitted that Taiwan was part of China but was still promising to protect it against Chinese aggression. In 1977 President Jimmy Carter revived talks with China, and in December 1978 the two nations reached an agreement: The United States would no longer defend Taiwan, but it would continue to sell it weapons so it could defend itself against China.

China and the United States resumed full diplomatic relations on January 1, 1979. Later that month Deng became the first Chinese leader to visit the United States in three decades. Deng's nine-day visit began January 28, when he flew to Washington, D.C., to meet with Carter. During the trip, Deng

A North Vietnamese soldier guards a captured Chinese tank man during the Chinese invasion of North Vietnam in 1979. The Chinese army was embarrassed and suffered forty-six thousand casualties.

charmed people he met with his gracious manners: He kissed children who sang in Chinese to honor him at a reception in Washington, and in Texas he donned a big cowboy hat and posed for photographers.

But Deng also showed the tough side of his nature during the trip. Although Deng said China would use peaceful means to be reunited with Taiwan, he admitted it might use other methods if they failed. Deng also made this unsettling comment: "The world today is far from tranquil. There are not only threats to peace, but the factors causing war are visibly growing."[98] Deng was commenting on neighboring Vietnam.

North Vietnam and South Vietnam had become one nation in 1975 after the U.S. government withdrew troops that had been supporting South Vietnam. Within a few years, however, Vietnam began fighting with neighboring Cambodia over territory both claimed. Vietnam invaded Cambodia in late 1978 and easily conquered it. This angered China, which supported Cambodia in the dispute. On February 17, 1979, just one week after Deng's historic visit to the United States, a Chinese force of 250,000 soldiers armed with tanks, airplanes, and artillery invaded Vietnam. The Chinese army withdrew on March 5 after only seventeen days of fighting. Deng had wanted to show the Vietnamese that China was more powerful and warn them that "they could not run about as much as they desired."[99] It was a painful lesson to deliver, however, as China suffered forty-six thousand casualties (soldiers killed, wounded, or missing).

Except for Vietnam, China's diplomatic relations with other nations under Deng were peaceful. One of them even righted a wrong that had angered the Chinese for more than a century. In the 1840s Great Britain had used its military superiority to force China to grant it leases for Chinese territory, including the island of Hong Kong and part of southern China. The leases were due to expire after June 30, 1997. The two nations began negotiating in 1982 on how to handle the exchange of land, and on December 19, 1984, they signed an agreement.

In what was called a "One Country, Two Systems" arrangement, China said it would let Hong Kong's capitalist financial system continue. It also promised to allow Hong Kong residents to continue to have the same rights and freedoms they had under British rule. Deng was willing to allow non-Communist conditions because "there was no other alternative."[100] He knew there would be trouble, maybe even a war with the British, if China had tried to change Hong Kong's capitalist, democratic lifestyle overnight.

Deng, however, was still not ready to give people in China the rights he had granted Hong Kong residents. Deng still distrusted democracy and thought it could hurt China.

Beijing Spring

When Deng liberalized China's economy and became friendly with capitalist nations, he allowed the Chinese more personal freedom. He loosened censorship over movies, plays, and music to allow people to express ideas other than Communist themes officials had demanded in the past, such as the need for people to sacrifice themselves for the nation. He allowed students to study in foreign countries to learn advances in science and technology. The new freedom even expressed itself in fashion. Men and women traded in their Mao suits—the drab-colored, collarless coat and pants Mao made popular—for clothing with brighter colors and more interesting styles. This period of greater freedom in the late 1970s became known as the Beijing Spring because new lifestyles were growing.

The CCP also encouraged people to criticize society and expose government problems, such as corruption by public officials. In November 1978 wall posters, a traditional Chinese form of political expression, appeared in many cities, including on the Democracy Wall in Beijing near the Forbidden City. The posters criticized officials for not allowing citizens more freedom and for failing to help citizens who were still poor. People also wrote articles with similar messages. In the January 29, 1979, edition of the underground periodical

Pride in Owning Land

In 1979 Steven W. Mosher lived for a year in a village in Guangdong Province in the People's Republic of China to study how rural Chinese lived. He explains how excited people were when the government allowed them to own land again:

Many years of ruthless condemnation of "the capitalist road" of material incentives and private profits failed to quench the entrepreneurial spirit of the Chinese, which flared anew once opportunity presented itself. "The first thing I'll do when I get my own mulberry patch," one excited [village] woman gushed to me when she first heard about the new program, "is plant beans between the rows of trees. You can't do that now because people are careless when they work. They would step on them when they are spreading [fertilizer] or picking mulberry leaves. But I'll be careful because they'll be mine." She went on to detail to me how she and her family would more efficiently manage the 2-acre mini-farm of fish pond, mulberry patch, and sugarcane field that would be theirs to till.

Steven W. Mosher, *Broken Earth: The Rural Chinese.* New York: Free, 1983, pp. 43–44.

Explorations, former Red Guard Wei Jingsheng argued that "if China wants to accomplish the Four Modernizations, it must first get rid of [strict government control of society]. People will become their own masters with democracy and human rights."[101]

Deng reacted to such criticism the same way Mao had in 1957 after his hundred flowers campaign ignited challenges to Communist authority. Officials in early 1979 began arresting Wei and other people who had criticized the government. Wei was sentenced to fifteen years in prison on phony charges that he gave state secrets to foreign journalists. As Deng had hoped, the political repression broke the budding drive for democracy by making people too afraid to challenge the government. Deng feared democracy would weaken or destroy Communist rule. He claimed that "talk about democracy in the abstract will inevitably [lead to] anarchy, to the complete disruption of political stability and unity, and to the total failure of our modernization program. If this happens [China] will once again be plunged into chaos, division, retrogression and darkness, and the Chinese people will be deprived of all hope."[102]

Only a decade later, however, another democracy movement arose. This one led to an even more brutal government reaction.

The Tiananmen Square Massacre

On January 6, 1989, Fang Lizhi, a noted scientist, asked Deng to free Wei and other people who had been jailed for criticizing the government. His daring request was ignored. However, it was symbolic of the growing desire many Chinese had for more personal freedom. The government still punished critics of Communism and denied citizens basic rights that people in other countries had, from freedom of expression to the right to religious worship. Many other people were also angry about corrupt public officials who took bribes, favoritism toward children of CCP officials, and poor conditions in Chinese universities.

On April 15 former CCP secretary-general Hu Yaobang died. University students and other people angry about all those issues decided to use his death to attack the government because he had favored many of the liberal policies they backed. The protests began with wall posters—a form of dissent the government had banned since 1980—and the first of many marches and rallies was held in Tiananmen Square on April 17. The protests continued in Tiananmen and spread to other cities, which embarrassed Chinese officials because they were reported worldwide.

Deng and other officials wanted to end the Tiananmen protest peacefully to preserve their new, more moderate international image. But when CCP officials met on May 17, Deng was furious that tens of thousands of protesters were defying the government, and at one point he yelled, "The minority yields to the majority!"[103] On May 20 the PRC declared martial law and sent

Student protesters place a barricade in front of a burning army vehicle during the July 4, 1989, pro-democracy demonstrations in Tiananmen Square.

soldiers to evict protesters from Tiananmen Square. Workers and citizens rallied around the protesters, erecting blockades and keeping the army from making them leave.

The PRC finally ran out of patience. On June 3, at 4:00 P.M., officials warned protest leaders that the army was preparing to attack and that protesters might be killed if they did not leave. Several hundred thousand people fled, but an estimated fifty thousand students and one hundred thousand other people stayed. In the early hours of June 4, tanks and thousands of soldiers

entered the square and began killing people. Tanks crushed protesters, and soldiers shot them. Chiang Yanyong, a doctor who treated some of the victims, claimed that the soldiers acted in "a frenzied fashion, using tanks, machine guns, and other weapons to suppress the totally unarmed students and citizens, killing innocent students."[104]

The fighting in Tiananmen ended quickly, but violence spread throughout Beijing the next two days as angry residents battled soldiers who had killed unarmed civilians. No one knows how many people died before the violence

The Tiananmen
Square Massacre

The Tiananmen Square Massacre was violent. Immanuel C.Y. Hsu, author of China Without Mao: The Search for a New Order, *describes some of the violence that occurred in that incident:*

Tanks, armored vehicles, and soldiers with automatic weapons struck from three directions in strict accordance with prearranged plans. In the early hours of June 4, thirty-five heavy tanks charged into the main encampment [of protesters in Tiananmen Square], crushing those students who were still inside. [Soldiers] and military police stormed out of [a building], their automatic weapons firing bullets, using electric cattle prods, rubber truncheons, and other types of special weapons, while tanks and armored vehicles rode roughshod through the scores of terror-stricken demonstrators. Eleven students—two from Beijing University and nine from Qinghua University—linked hands in a symbolic gesture to protect [a statue of] the Goddess of Democracy; they were mowed down with the statue. By 6 a.m. those who could had already escaped, while the dead or maimed were scattered all over the blood-soaked killing field. The soldiers hurriedly bulldozed the bodies into large piles for burning on the spot or packed them in plastic bags for cremation outside the city. The carnage was over in seven hours.

Immanuel C.Y. Hsu, *China Without Mao: The Search for a New Order.* New York: Oxford University Press, 1990, p. 289.

A lone Chinese student blocks a line of tanks during the Tiananmen Square demonstrations. The man was later executed by the Chinese government.

ended. The PRC claims the number of dead or injured was two hundred to three hundred, but some Western newspapers reported the figure was twice as high, and Chinese student groups and the Chinese Red Cross have claimed it was ten times the PRC estimate.

Deng's Prediction

Although Deng's legacy is tainted by his opposition to democracy, he helped most Chinese have a better life. In 1991 Deng said he hoped his economic policies would be successful enough to quiet people who were still criticizing him for violating Communist ideals.

According to Deng, "If we can reach a comfortable standard of living by the end of this century, then that will wake them up a bit. And in the next century when we, as a socialist country, join the middle ranks of the developed nations, that will help to convince them. Most of these people will genuinely see that they were mistaken."[105]

Deng's prediction was too modest. By the end of the twentieth century China had one of the world's strongest economies, and by then experts were predicting that in the next century it would become the world's dominant economic power.

Chapter Seven

China Today: A Troubled Economic Giant

On October 1, 2007, the People's Republic of China celebrated the fifty-eighth anniversary of its founding. The night before, at a reception in Beijing, premier Wen Jiabao boasted about how much the nation had accomplished in its short history. However, Wen also warned that China faced many challenges in the future:

> Tremendous changes have taken place in our country. The road of socialism with Chinese characteristics we have taken is a broad road of making the people prosperous and the country strong and of the rejuvenation of the Chinese nation. We have already made great achievements [but] on the road ahead, there are both opportunities and challenges.[106]

The phrase "socialism with Chinese characteristics" is shorthand for the reforms Deng Xiaoping initiated to make China's economy a hybrid of Communism and capitalism. By 2008 those changes had enabled China to develop the world's second-biggest economy—only the United States economy was larger—and to transform the way people lived as radically as Mao Zedong had when he made China Communist.

The Chinese today still ask each other when they meet, "Ni chi fan le mei yo?" which in English means, "Have you eaten yet?"[107] That traditional greeting stems from the poverty that plagued China for centuries and sometimes caused widespread famine that killed millions of people. The answer today is almost always "yes" because China's thirty-year economic boom has lifted 400 million Chinese out of poverty. What is more surprising is that they may have eaten a McDonald's hamburger. China, which once condemned Western culture, has embraced it. American food, rock music, and fashions are all popular in China. In October 2007 the designer label Fendi held a fashion show in China and used the Great Wall as a runway for models to showcase its latest styles.

Life in China is much better than it was three decades ago because of its unparalleled economic growth. However, the nation also faces major problems, such as a growing disparity of wealth between rich and working-class Chinese and the desire people have for more freedom.

China's Economic Miracle

China's economic boom slowed for several years after the Tiananmen Square Massacre because the United States and other countries were wary of dealing with a nation that used violence to stop political protests. But revulsion over the massacre faded and foreign countries resumed doing business with China.

In the three decades after Deng began his reforms in 1978, China's economy grew an average of 10 percent each year, a rate that is believed to be greater than any country in history has experienced over such an extended period. Most growth was driven by the manufacture of products China made for export to other countries, including toys, clothing, shoes, and golf clubs. They were produced in partnership with foreign companies such as Nike, Disney, and Mattel, which built factories in China to take advantage of its cheap, plentiful labor force. Between 1978 and 1993, the value of such products increased from 20.65 billion to 195.8 billion, and

the biggest purchaser was the United States.

The income the exports created has transformed China. One of China's richest regions today is Guangdong Province, site of one of the first special economic zones. In 1978 Melinda Liu and other journalists from nearby Hong Kong were invited to Shenzhen for a ground-breaking ceremony for the new zone. Liu said she and other journalists had trouble believing that the small fishing village, with only a handful of families, "was supposed to be China's future." Liu returned in 2007 to find how much Shenzhen had changed: "Thirty years later Shenzhen is a metropolis of 12 million people, and still growing. The huts have been replaced by rank upon rank of office blocks, like the 69-story Shun Hing Plaza, currently the world's seventh tallest building at 1,260 feet."[108]

China's economy also expanded through greater yields in agriculture due to mechanization—tractors and not humans now pull plows—and more scientific ways to grow crops. The Chinese economy also swelled considerably—and easily—on July 1, 1997, when Hong Kong reverted to Chinese control. The return of Hong Kong made the Chinese proud because it erased the insult of having been forced to surrender it to the British 150 years earlier. More importantly, it increased China's economic strength because Hong Kong was one of Asia's main centers for banking, manufacturing, and shipping. China also benefited from investment by Hong Kong

A modern steel-smelting furnace in Taiyuan, China, is a testimony to China's rapid economic growth in the more than three decades since Nixon's visit.

firms—from 1997 to 2005, Hong Kong companies invested more than $240 billion in mainland businesses. As a result Hong Kong, which has a population of 6.9 million, employed more than 12 million people in China.

Journalist Fareed Zakaria believes China's economic transformation was the fastest in history. In a 2008 article, Zakaria wrote, "In three decades China experienced the same degree of industrialization, urbanization and social transformation as Europe did in two centuries."[109] Equally fast and dramatic has been the change in the way China's people live.

Economic Growth Transforms Lives

Visitors from Western nations are still amazed at the virtual rivers of bicycles that flow through China's cities. Although the bicycle is still China's most common form of transportation, auto ownership tripled from 2002 to 2008 as more people had enough money to buy a car. The number of automobiles is still small compared with those of Western nations—in 2008 Beijing, a city of 16 million people, had about 3 million cars—but they are transforming the lives of their owners. Zhu Chao explained in 2008 what owning a car meant to him: "I really like what the car brings to my life—convenience, freedom, flexibility. I can't imagine life without it."[110]

Many changes in daily life have occurred because of China's close ties with nations it does business with. Communist leaders once condemned blue jeans and rock and roll as symbols of capitalist decadence. Today they allow the Chinese to enjoy Western culture, and that has altered life in many ways, including what people eat and drink. Tea is China's traditional beverage. But Li Mei, a freelance writer, regularly visits one of Beijing's many Starbucks cafés, which feature coffee. "I could stay at Starbucks for the entire day,"[111] Li admits. And many Chinese who once lunched on rice or a bowl of noodles now eat a hamburger and fries.

The jobs people hold have also changed due to economic growth and new technology. Zhao Zijian works in Beijing as a computer programmer. Zhao also has another job, one that symbolizes the new cultural freedom the Chinese have—he plays lead guitar in a rock band called Hedgehog. For decades Chinese officials would not allow people to listen to such music. But Liu Lixin, a member of the rock band Ordnance, says that, in 2008, "Beijing is paradise for rock musicians and fans."[112]

The lifestyle changes have been greatest in big cities, where there are more good jobs. But in some areas of the country, millions of Chinese still struggle to have a decent life.

Unequal Economic Growth

Farmers in rural areas were the earliest beneficiaries of Deng's economic policies. By 1983 Yang Jingli had earned enough money from farming his own land in Fengyang County to build a new home. "When have peasants ever dreamed of owning two-story houses?" Yang asked. "In all history [in China] there hasn't been anything like this."[113] But farmers began to struggle financially in later years as crop prices fell and expenses rose. In 2000 Yixian farmer Chen Wenjun said, "After all I pay for taxes, fertilizer, and water, I'm lucky if I can break even. If prices go down even more, I'm not sure we'll be able to survive."[114] Chen had to work part time at a printing factory to feed his family.

In 2008 about 800 million people—70 percent of China's population—still lived in rural areas and about 80 percent of them had trouble making enough money to survive. The bleak financial situation had existed for several decades, forcing men and women to leave home and seek jobs elsewhere. China had an estimated 130 million transient laborers in 2008. Most of them found work, but some wound up begging to survive. In 2005 U.S. journalist Raymond A. Schroth said a man in dirty clothes followed him into his

Some Still Live Primitively

In 2003 journalist Charlie Cook visited Xibaipo, a remote mountain village some 600 miles (966km) southeast of Beijing. He described typical primitive homes built of stone or brick that could house three generations of the same family:

Most houses have two doorways opening onto a courtyard that is surrounded by a six-foot stone or concrete wall. In the courtyard, chickens run loose, and a couple of pigs may be rooting around in a pen ringed by stones or dug into a hillside. Few houses have outside doors. Instead, residents hang blankets in the doorway and pull them aside for ventilation. Cooking is done over an open fire. The only obvious sign that we weren't seeing a Chinese village of 200 years ago was that every house seemed to have a refrigerator, a television, and, up on the roof, a rusting satellite dish. Everyone seemed to live in the village and to farm nearby plots of land, some smaller than a putting green. The people cultivate every available flat or nearly flat arable patch, and on the houses' flat roofs, they spread corn to dry, still on the cob.

Charlie Cook, "Standing on the Brink of the Chinese Century," *National Journal*, November 8, 2003, p. 38.

Shanghai hotel and asked for money, saying, "I have no work."[115]

The migrant labor force exists because most economic development has occurred in urban areas and special economic zones. Economic growth has also been unequal geographically because powerful Chinese Communist Party and government officials used their authority to stimulate growth in their communities. And when Deng allowed people to own companies, many party members used their positions to enrich themselves by starting businesses. In 2008 Yang Guowen led one of the largest companies in Yiwu, a global production center for inexpensive items like playing cards and sunglasses. The firm was begun in 1987 by his father, who was Yiwu's mayor and is now a member of China's People's Congress.

Yang is a symbol of the huge income gap that exists between businessmen and workers. Yang drives a BMW 760I that workers in his plant would have to work a lifetime to buy. He also represents another problem in Chinese society—he is a "princeling," the derisive term for children of party and government officials. They are called princelings because their families are so wealthy and they receive so much preferential treatment that they are like members of a royal family. Li Ruihan is one of many Communist officials who believe that such income disparity and social inequality could lead to serious trouble: "If you get on their wrong side [average people], it doesn't matter who you are, you're done for. As the saying goes, 'the water can carry the boat, but it can also sink it.'"[116] Ironically, the Communist revolution was fueled by the hatred average people had for the wealthy elite of the past.

Income disparity and social inequality are major problems for China. An issue that is potentially even more serious is the growing desire Chinese people have for democracy.

China's Limited Democracy

On June 4, 1998, the ninth anniversary of the Tiananmen Square Massacre, Bao Tong publicly declared that "June 4 [1989] is a tragedy for the entire country and the entire Chinese race."[117] In 1989 Tong was a high-ranking Communist official who tried to get Deng to negotiate with demonstrators instead of using force to disperse them. Tong served seven years in prison for seeming to side with the protesters.

The fact that Tong was not punished for his comment nine years later indicates the greater freedom China has granted its citizens in the nearly two decades since the Tiananmen Square Massacre. Chinese people today can work where they want instead of having to stay at one job their entire life. They travel freely in China and even to foreign countries, and they own property and businesses. They can also practice

Zeng Jinyan, activist, meets with reporters to relate her experiences blogging about issues such as AIDS and population growth. The Chinese government controls all access to the Internet.

the religion of their choice, something the Communists once tried to prohibit.

This freedom, however, is limited. Communist leaders often punish people who criticize the government in speeches, printed articles, or Internet blogs. The Communists especially fear the Internet because it is an easy way for people who oppose them to communicate and spread ideas. Chinese officials tightly control and monitor the Internet and sometimes physically intimidate people to make them stop using it.

Zeng Jinyan writes a daily blog and campaigns for the rights of people with acquired immune deficiency syndrome (AIDS), an illness officials hate to admit even exists in China. In 2007 officers began spying on Zeng and her husband by following them when they left home. One day, as the couple walked in a park, Zeng confronted them: "I looked back at the state security officers whose keys were rattling at their waists, and I said to them, 'Aren't you ashamed? Keep further away from us!'"[118]

Zeng was also targeted by officials for blogging about being pregnant. Because China limits families to one child to control its population even though many people want more children, it frowns on anyone who openly discusses the joys of being pregnant and having a child. The one-child policy began in 1979 because China's population was growing so fast that officials feared the nation would be unable to feed or economically sustain so many people. At the time, Vice Premier Chen Muhua

said, "[Communism] should make it possible to regulate the reproduction of human beings."[119] Chinese officials still punish people who have more than one child by making them pay a fine and by denying them government benefits, including free education for their children. Rich people and party members, however, often ignore the one-child policy.

The one-child prohibition is one of the most potent symbols of China's lack of freedom. Li Datong was editor of *Freezing Point*, a weekly newspaper that ran stories about government corruption and other problems, until government officials fired him in January 2006. Li would like to see democracy come to China, but he believes that will take a long time because Communists do not want to surrender their one-party control of the nation. Li says, "We have to be patient. I don't think the government will loosen controls by itself."[120]

China's Leaders Today

Comments that Hu Jintao, China's president and CCP secretary-general, made on October 15, 2007, at the opening meeting of the CCP National Congress showed how unready Chinese officials are to give people more freedom. Hu said the word democracy more than sixty times in his two-and-half-hour speech, but he was careful to note that he meant democracy "with Chinese characteristics," which meant democracy conducted under the "leadership of the Communist Party."[121] Although Hu and other leaders continue to ignore

Confusion over Written Chinese

In 1979 China began a policy of limiting families to one child to control its rapidly growing population. Officials often coerce women who have a child and become pregnant again to have an abortion. Historian Steven W. Mosher, who lived in the People's Republic of China for a year from 1979 until 1980, describes how a Communist Party official tried to bully pregnant women to have abortions:

There were eighteen women, all [pregnant and] many red-eyed from lack of sleep and crying. They sat listlessly on short plank benches [while] He Kaifeng explained the purpose of the meeting in no uncertain terms. "You are here because you have yet to 'think clear' about birth control, and you will remain here until you do." He spoke to the women with an ease that bespoke many years of experience in mass meetings, but his message to the women was anything but reassuring. "China must develop, and we will gradually develop into a strong socialist state," he continued, "but whether or not we develop depends on controlling our population."

Steven W. Mosher, *Broken Earth: The Rural Chinese*. New York: Free Press, 1984, p. 225.

the desire of the Chinese people for democracy, they have begun to listen to their concerns about some issues.

Hu's first speech after being elected secretary-general in 2002 dealt with social inequality. On December 6, 2002, in the poor village of Xibaipo in Hebei Province, Hu said officials should quit trying to become rich and concentrate on helping average people: "Only by upholding plain living and hard struggle can we wholeheartedly attain the aim of serving the people."[122] During Hu's tenure, China has punished party officials who tried to become rich through stealing government funds and other types of corruption.

In 2007 the government even admitted that it had made mistakes on the biggest construction project in its history. Three Gorges Dam, which spans the Yangtze River and is the largest dam in the world, was completed in 2006 after more than a decade of construction. Built to limit seasonal flooding and provide an environmentally friendly source of electricity, it was controversial because it forced 4 million people to move. Since its completion, there have been problems with water quality, and landslides have killed people. On September 26, 2007, the Xinhua news agency warned that structural problems might cause more

Giant construction cranes working in Beijing are indicative of China's rising economic power.

landslides: "If no preventive measures are taken, the project could lead to catastrophe."[123] Xinhua, a government-run news organization, quoted officials who had worked on the project. It is highly unusual for Chinese officials to admit mistakes. The public comments were considered a way to calm millions of people who were angry about the dam.

Wen Jiabao has also shown a willingness to respond to public concerns. He has been praised for trying to help rural agricultural workers and laborers who are struggling financially. Wen, however, believes the best way to do that is for China to continue its friendly relations with other nations so its economy can continue to grow. In his speech on the eve of Communist China's fifty-eighth anniversary, Wen said, "We must take the road of peaceful development, implement the opening up strategy of mutual benefit and win-win results, maintain world peace, and promote common development."[124] Once considered a military threat to capitalist nations like the United States, China now only wants to be their trading and investment partner.

The Chinese Century?

In the twenty-first century, economic strength is more important than military might in making a nation powerful. China's economy grew so much in the 1990s that when the twenty-first century began in 2000, many people began to speculate that China would eventually have the world's most powerful economy. In a 2003 story assessing China's future, journalist Charlie Cook said China had already become so strong that it would influence events around the world for decades to come.

"China will likely transform the era," Cook wrote. "We may soon be living in the Chinese Century."[125]

Many people around the world agree with that assessment. In 2007 the Chicago Council on Global Affairs and WorldPublicOpinion.org polled people in fourteen countries. The results showed that a majority of citizens in eight countries expect China will one day have a larger economy than the United States. The poll also showed that people are unconcerned China will have such power. "Suddenly, the Chinese dragon doesn't look so scary,"[126] writes journalist George Wehrfritz.

The selection of China to host the 2008 Summer Olympics in Beijing was yet

A Young Businesswoman

Li Qinghe owns a small shop in Suzhou that sells Chinese crafts and jewelry she makes. Li explains how different her life is from that of her parents:

"My parents were astonished when I told them I wanted to open a shop. My father's a Chinese teacher and my mother's a nurse, and both are still working hard. They would never have thought of doing anything like this themselves." [Li] is aware that she has a degree of freedom unimagined by her parents, not only in being able to start her own business, but also in having the time and resources to study for [an advanced degree] in film animation. Sometimes Li closes her shop for a few days just to go traveling, and she's currently considering a trip abroad. "When my parents were working hard to support the family, they had no time to think whether freedom was precious to them or not." She laughs: "Sometimes I'm dissatisfied with what I have simply because I am free enough to be able to think about it."

Alison Bailey et al., *China: People, Place, Culture, History*. New York: DK, 2007, p. 216.

another sign of the many changes that have occurred in China since its founding and its new and improved world image. That world image, however, was damaged in early 2008 when violence flared in Tibet, the neighboring country China had invaded and conquered a half century earlier. Officials in many countries criticized China in March 2008 for brutally repressing protests by Tibetans who were demanding greater freedom.

Supporters of Tibet's bid for more independence protested against the 2008 Beijing Olympics. The violent confrontations with Tibetans resurrected old fears about the Chinese government's past use of force against citizens who opposed government policies such as the Tiananmen Square Massacre. The violence left people to wondering how China will affect the rest of the world as it keeps growing in power in the coming century.

Notes

Introduction: China's Continuing Revolution

1. Quoted in Jonathan D. Spence, *The Search for Modern China*. New York: Norton, 1990, p. 577.

2. Quoted in Jung Chang and Jon Halliday, *Mao: The Unknown Story*. New York: Knopf, 2004, p. 15.

3. C.K. Yang, *A Chinese Village in Early Communist Transition*. Cambridge, MA: Technology, 1959, p. 204.

4. Quoted in Stephen Endicott, *Red Earth: Revolution in a Sichuan Village*. New York: New Amsterdam, 1991, p. 4.

5. Quoted in Harrison Salisbury, *China: 100 Years of Revolution*. New York: Holt, Rinehart, and Winston, 1983, p. 211.

6. Quoted in *BBC Monitoring Asia Pacific*, "Text of Chinese Premier's Speech at National Day Reception," October 1, 2007, p. 1.

7. Quoted in Catherine Sampson, "China Trembles at the Power of the Blog," *Independent* (London), August 6, 2007. p. 1.

Chapter One: The Communists Conquer China

8. Mao Zedong, "The Chinese People Have Stood Up!" September 21, 1949, UCLA Center for East Asian Studies. www.international.ucla. edu /eas/documents/mao490921.html.

9. Quoted in Chang and Halliday, *Mao*, p. 322.

10. Quoted in Alison Bailey et al., *China: People, Place, Culture, History*. New York: DK, 2007, p. 113.

11. Quoted in Spence, *The Search for Modern China*, p. 236.

12. Quoted in Salisbury, *China*, p. 44.

13. Quoted in Edgar Snow, *Red Star over China*. New York: Random House, 1938, p. 398.

14. Quoted in Stuart R. Schram, *Mao Tse-tung*. New York: Simon & Schuster, 1966, p. 19.

15. Quoted in Richard Hooker, "Mao Tse-Tung," Washington State University. www.wsu.edu:8080/~dee/ MODCHINA/MAO.HTM.

16. Quoted in Spence, *The Search for Modern China*, p. 75.

17. Quoted in Salisbury, *China*, p. 165.

18. Quoted in Edgar Snow, *Edgar Snow's China: A Personal Account of the Chinese Revolution Compiled from the Writings of Edgar Snow*. New York: Random House, 1981, p. 218.

19. Quoted in Snow, *Red Star over China*, p. 239.

20. Mao Tse-tung, "On the Chungking Negotiations (October 17, 1945)," Art Bin. http://art-bin.com/art/omaotoc.html.

21. Quoted in Richard Cavendish, "Septembers Past," *History Today*, September 1999, p. 52.

Chapter Two: China Becomes a Communist Nation

22. Mao Tse-tung "Report on an Investigation of the Peasant Movement in Hunan (March 1927)," Art Bin. http://art-bin.com/art/omaotoc.html.

23. Quote in UCLA Center for East Asian Studies, "Conversation Between the Soviet Union's Joseph Stalin and China's Mao Zedong, December 16, 1949." www.isop.ucla.edu/eas/documents/mao491216.html.

24. Quoted in John Gittings, *China Changes Face: The Road from Revolution, 1949–1989*. New York: Oxford University Press, 1989, p. 23.

25. Quoted in Snow, *Edgar Snow's China*, p. 45.

26. Quoted in Endicott, *Red Earth*, p. 22.

27. Quoted in Spence, *The Search for Modern China*, p. 492.

28. Quoted in Salisbury, *China*, p. 199.

29. Quoted in J.A.G. Roberts, *Modern China: An Illustrated History*. Gloucestershire, England: Sutton, 1998, p. 229.

30. Quoted in Maurice Meisner, *Mao's China: A History of the People's Republic*. New York: Free Press, 1977, p. 228.

31. Quoted in J.A.G. Roberts, *A Concise History of China*. Cambridge, MA: Harvard University Press, 1999, p. 267.

32. Quoted in Endicott, *Red Earth*, p. 57.

33. Quoted in Steven W. Mosher, *Broken Earth: The Rural Chinese*. New York: Free Press, 1984, p. 266.

34. Quoted in Franz Shurman and Orville Shell, eds., *Communist China: Revolutionary Reconstruction and International Confrontation, 1949–1966*. New York: Vintage, 1966, p. 462.

35. Quoted in Immanuel C.Y. Hsu, *The Rise of Modern China*, 3rd ed. New York: Oxford University Press, 1983, p. 695.

36. Quoted in Meisner, *Mao's China*, p. 245.

Chapter Three: China Becomes a Military and Political Power

37. Mao, "The Chinese People Have Stood Up!"

38. Hsu, *The Rise of Modern China*, p. 662.

39. Quoted in Chang and Halliday, *Mao*, p. 452.

40. Quoted in Spence, *The Search for Modern China*, p. 525.

41. Quoted in Hsu, *The Rise of Modern China*, p. 662.

42. Quoted in Chang and Halliday, *Mao*, p. 353.

43. Quoted in John Toland, *In Mortal Combat: Korea, 1950–1953*. New York: William Morrow, 1991, p. 235.

44. Quoted in Stanley Weintraub, *MacArthur's War: Korea and the Undoing of an American Hero*. New York: Free Press, 2000, p. 176.

45. Quoted in Toland, *In Mortal Combat*, p. 236.

46. Mao Zedong, "Order to the Chinese People's Volunteers," October 1950, UCLA East Asian Studies Documents. www.isop.ucla.edu/eas/documents/mao501008.html.

47. Quoted in Philip Short, *Mao: A Life*. New York: Henry Holt, 1999, p. 432.

48. Quoted in David Rees, ed., *The Korean War: History and Tactics*. New York: Crescent, 1984, p. 124.

49. Quoted in Qiang Zhai, *China and the Vietnam Wars, 1950–1975*. Chapel Hill: University of North Carolina Press, 2000, p. 58.

50. Quoted in Hsu, *The Rise of Modern China*, p. 703.

51. Quoted in Qiang, *China and the Vietnam Wars*, p. 220.

52. Quoted in Spence, *The Search for Modern China*, p. 527.

53. Quoted in Michael D. Pixley, "Eisenhower's Strategy in the Taiwan Strait Drove a Wedge Between the Soviet Union and China," *Military History*, February 2005, p. 16.

54. Quoted in Chang and Halliday, *Mao*, p. 485.

Chapter Four: China's Continuous Revolution

55. Quoted in Stuart R. Schram, *The Political Thought of Mao Tse-tung*. New York: Praeger, 1963, p. 253.

56. Quoted in C.K. Yang, *The Chinese Family in the Communist Revolution*. Cambridge, MA: Technology, 1959, p. 178.

57. Quoted in Short, *Mao*, p. 460.

58. Quoted in Salisbury, *China*, p. 202.

59. Quoted in Jonathan D. Spence, *The Gate of Heavenly Peace: The Chinese and Their Revolution, 1895–1980*. New York: Viking, 1981, p. 332.

60. Quoted in Roberts, *Modern China*, p. 233.

61. Quoted in Art Bin, "Quotations from Chairman Mao Tse-tung." http://art-bin.com/art/omaotoc.html.

62. Quoted in Meisner, *Mao's China*, p. 310.

63. Quoted in Salisbury, *China*, p. 211.

64. Quoted in Schram, *Mao Tse-tung*, p. 310.

65. Quoted in Ji-Li Chiang, "Troubling Times in China," *National Geographic World*, June 2000, p. 24.

66. Quoted in Jonathan D. Spence, *Mao Zedong*. New York: Penguin Putnam, 1999, p. 166.

67. Asia Research Centre, ed., *The Great Cultural Revolution in China*. Rutland, VT: C.E. Tuttle, 1968, p. 398.

68. Quoted in Chang and Halliday, *Mao*, p. 519.

69. Quoted in Hsu, *The Rise of Modern China*, p. 706.

70. Quoted in Chihua Wen, *The Red Mirror: Children of China's Cultural Revolution*. San Francisco: CAL Westview, 1995, p. 25.

71. Quoted in Ross Terrill, *Mao: A Biography*. New York: Harper & Row, p. 329.

Chapter Five: The Struggle for Power Continues

72. Quoted in Jonathan D. Spence, "Mao Zedong," *Time*. www.time.com/time/time100/leaders/profile/mao.html.

73. Quoted in Hsu, *The Rise of Modern China*, p. 712.

74. Asia Research Centre, ed., *The Great Cultural Revolution in China*, p. 398.

75. Quoted in Harrison E. Salisbury, *The New Emperors: China in the Era of Mao and Deng*. Boston: Little, Brown, 1992, p. 294.

76. Quoted in Hsu, *The Rise of Modern China*, p. 719.

77. Quoted in Meisner, *Mao's China*, p. 370.

78. Quoted in Jeffrey A. Bader, "China After Deng Xiaoping: Prospects for Continuity or Change," *Asian Affairs: An American Review*, Summer 1997, p. 69.

79. Quoted in Richard Evans, *Deng Xiaoping and the Making of Modern China*. New York: Viking, 1993, p. 205.

80. Quoted in Margaret MacMillan, *Nixon and Mao: The Week That Changed the World*. New York: Random House, 2007, p. 31.

81. Quoted in Spence, *The Search for Modern China*, p. 631.

82. Quoted in Hsu, *The Rise of Modern China*, p. 741.

83. Quoted in UCLA Center for East Asian Studies, East Asian Studies Documents, "Joint Communiqué of the United States of America and the People's Republic of China, February 28, 1972." www.isop.ucla.edu/eas/documents/Shanghai.html.

84. Quoted in Spence, *Mao Zedong*, p. 174.

85. Quoted in Salisbury, *China*, p. 244.

86. Quoted in Norm Goldstein, ed., *China: From the Long March to Tiananmen Square*. New York: Henry Holt, 1990, p. 143.

87. Quoted in Immanuel C.Y. Hsu, *China Without Mao: The Search for a New Order*. New York: Oxford University Press, 1990, p. 11.

88. Quoted in Goldstein, ed., *China*, p. 143.

89. Quoted in Short, *Mao*, p. 627.

90. Quoted in Hsu, *China Without Mao*, p. 137.

91. Quoted in Hsu, *China Without Mao*, p. 147.

Chapter Six: Deng Xiaoping Leads China in a New Direction

92. Quoted in Gittings, *China Changes Face*, p. 39.

93. Quoted in Roberts, *A Concise History of China*, p. 290.

94. Quoted in Kwan Ha Yim, ed., *China Since Mao*. New York: Facts On File, 1980, p. 43.

95. Quoted in Hsu, *The Rise of Modern China*, p. 804.

96. Quoted in Peter Nolan, *China at the Crossroads*. Cambridge, UK: Polity, 2004, p. 7.

97. Quoted in William Hinton, *The Great Reversal: The Privatization of China, 1978–1989*. New York: Monthly Review, 1990, p. 53.

98. Quoted in Hsu, *The Rise of Modern China*, p. 822.

99. Quoted in Hsu, *China Without Mao*, p. 78.

100. Quoted in Richard Evans, *Deng Xiaoping and the Making of Modern China*. New York: Viking Penguin, 1994, p. 271.

101. Quoted in Jonathan D. Spence, *The Gate of Heavenly Peace: The Chinese and Their Revolution, 1895–1980*. New York: Viking, 1981, p. 361.

102. Quoted in Nolan, *China at the Crossroads*, p. 72.

103. Quoted in Matthew Forney, "What Really Happened?" *Time*, January 15, 2001. www.time.com/time/asia /magazine/2001/0115/cover1.html.

104. Quoted in Jasper Becker, "Tiananmen Square, 15 Years On; Despite Its Booming Economy, China Is No Closer to Establishing Democracy than When the People's Liberation Army Massacred Protesting Students in Beijing in 1989," *Independent* (London), June 4, 2004, p. 26.

105. Quoted in Patrick E. Tyler, "Deng Xiaoping: A Political Wizard Who Put China on the Capitalist Road," *New York Times*, February 20, 1997, p. 1.

Chapter Seven: China Today: A Troubled Economic Giant

106. Quoted in *BBC Monitoring Asia Pacific*, "Wen Jiabao Speech at Reception Celebrating 58th Founding Anniversary of People's Republic of China (30 September 2007)," October 1, 2007, p. 1.

107. Quoted in Mosher, *Broken Earth*, p. 49.

108. Melinda Liu, "Mao to Now," *Newsweek*, January 7, 2008, p. 42.

109. Quoted in Fareed Zakaria, "The Rise of a Fierce Yet Fragile Superpower," *Newsweek*, January 7, 2008, p. 38.

110. Quoted in Maureen Fan, "Auto Mania Hits China," *Milwaukee Journal Sentinel*, January 22, 2008, p. A3.

111. Quoted in Lan Xinzhen, "The Charm of Starbucks," *Beijing Review*, December 22, 2006. www.bj review.com.cn/life/txt/2006-12/ 22/ content_51717.html.

112. Quoted in Yuan Yuan, "Rock On," *Beijing Review*, November 12, 2007. www.bjreview.com.cn/culture/ txt/2007-11/12/content_85235. html.

113. Quoted in Hinton, *The Great Reversal*, p. 48.

114. Quoted in Bay Fang, "Growing Troubles Down on the Farm," *U.S. News & World Report*, May 29, 2000, p. 40.

115. Quoted in Raymond A. Schroth, "The Streets of Shanghai," *Commonweal*, February 11, 2005, p. 39.

116. Quoted in Fintan O Toole, "Yang Guowen, Unequal Society," *Irish Times* (Dublin), November 18, 2006, p. 3.

117. Quoted in Kevin Platt, "Nine Years After Tiananmen, China's Leaders More Lenient," *Christian Science Monitor*, June 5, 1998, p. 1.

118. Quoted in Catherine Sampson, "China Trembles at the Power of the Blog," *Independent* (London), August 6, 2007, p. 1.

119. Quoted in Mosher, *Broken Earth*, p. 224.

120. Quoted in Melinda Liu, "Loosening Up 'Under Pressure,'" *Newsweek*, April 3, 2006, p. 58.

121. Quoted in Simon Elegant, "China's 'Democracy,'" *Time South Pacific*, October 29, 2007, p. 8.

122. Quoted in Nolan, *China at the Crossroads*, p. 170.

123. Quoted in Tim Johnson, "Trouble Flowing from Dam in China," *Milwaukee Journal Sentinel*, October 16, 2007, p. A4.

124. Quoted in *BBC Monitoring Asia Pacific*, "Wen Jiabao Speech at Reception Celebrating 58th Founding Anniversary of People's Republic of China (30 September 2007)," p. 1.

125. Quoted in Charlie Cook, "Standing on the Brink of the Chinese Century," *National Journal*, November 8, 2003, p. 40.

126. Quoted in George Wehrfritz, "Few Fear the Dragon," *Newsweek*, June 4, 2007, p. 34.

Glossary

capitalism: An economic system in which individuals profit from private ownership of factories, industries, businesses, and other economic means of production.

China: A generic name for the People's Republic of China.

Chinese Communist Party (CCP): The ruling party of the People's Republic of China.

civil war: A conflict in which groups wage a military fight for political control of a nation.

commune: An agricultural unit in which many people live and work together to farm a large area.

Communism: A totalitarian system of government in which the state owns and controls factories, industries, businesses, and other economic means of production and uses the profits from them for the common good of all citizens.

democracy: A system of government in which people wield power by electing officials to govern them.

dictator: Someone who has supreme power to govern a nation.

dynasty: A series of rulers of a nation descended from the same family.

mainland China: A nickname for the PRC.

People's Liberation Army (PLA): The national army of the People's Republic of China.

People's Republic of China (PRC): The official name for China.

red: A nickname for a Communist.

Republic of China (also known as Taiwan or Formosa): The democratic nation on the island of Taiwan that was formed after the Communists won control of China.

revolution: When one group uses military force to seize political control of a country; when a nation's leaders make drastic changes in the economic or social rules they use to govern.

socialism: Any economic or political system in which the state owns and controls factories, industries, businesses, and other economic means of production and uses the profits from them for the common good of all citizens; Communism is one form of socialism.

For Further Reading

Books

Jasper Becker, *Dragon Rising: An Inside Look at China Today*. Washington, DC: National Geographic Society, 2006. Excellent pictures accompany a well-written book about what China is like today.

Anne Faulkner, *Mao Zedong*. Austin, TX: Raintree Steck-Vaughn, 2003. A good biography for younger readers.

David M. Haugen, ed., *China*. Detroit: Greenhaven, 2006. This book includes viewpoints by various authors on economic, social, and other issues confronting China today.

David Pietrusza, *The Chinese Cultural Revolution*. San Diego: Lucent, 1997. A detailed look at the Cultural Revolution, from its causes to its aftermath.

Edward L. Shaughnessy, ed., *China: Empire and Civilization*. Oxford, NY: Oxford University Press, 2000. A history of China and how its culture has developed.

John Bryan Starr, *Understanding China: A Guide to China's Economy, History, and Political Structure*. New York: Hill and Wang, 2001. A comprehensive look at how China has evolved through many centuries of history.

Web Sites

Beijing Review (www.bjreview.com.cn/). The Web site of China's national English weekly newspaper has interesting articles and pictures on daily life in China, from politics and sports to features on popular culture.

China in the Twentieth Century (http://departments.kings.edu/history/20c/china.html). This Web site has detailed information on the history of China and the People's Republic of China.

China.org.cn (www.china.org.cn). This government-run Web site offers news and a wealth of basic information about Chinese history, politics, economics, and culture.

Virtual Museum of the "Cultural Revolution" (www.cnd.org/CR/english/). This site by *China News Digest*, which is located in Maryland, has detailed accounts, photographs, and documents that explain this important event in Chinese history.

Index

endorsement of, 52, 54
establishment of Chinese Soviet
    Republic by, 18
establishment of PRC by, 8
families of leaders of, 82–83
government in Yenan, 19, 22
government officials and
    appointment of, 24, 25–26
    complaints about, 74
    punishment of corrupt, 85
loyalty to families and, 47–48
    officials returned after, 60, 67, 68
organizations to further goals of,
    47
popularity of, 21
religion and, 47
Soviet Union and, 17
victory declared by, 13
world revolution and, 42
during World War II, 20–21
See also Communism; People's
    Liberation Army (PLA)
Chinese language, 15
Chinese Soviet Republic, 18
civil war, 18–20, 21–23
Cixi (empress), 16
clothing, 73
communes, 10–11, 30–31, 34, 50
Communism
    Deng and, 11, 69
    described, 9–10
    gradual transition to, 35–36
    status of women, 26
    See also Chinese Communist Party
        (CCP)
Communist People's Liberation Army
    (PLA). *See* People's Liberation Army
    (PLA)
Confucius, 26
Cook, Charlie, 82, 87

Cultural Revolution
    condemnation by, 65, 66
    ended by Mao, 55
    endorsement by, 52, 54
    families separated during, 48
    international isolation during, 60
    officials of, 60, 67, 68
    reasons for, 49–51
    Red Guard, 11, 51–55, 57, 60

dams, 31, 85–86
deforestation, 33
democracy
    current status of, 83–85
    under Deng, 73–74
    media control and, 48–49
    repression of, 11–12
    Tiananmen Square Massacre and,
        74–77
Democratic Republic of Vietnam
    (North Vietnam), 40–42, 72
Democratic Wall, 49
Deng Xiaoping
    criticism of
        by Mao, 51
        by promoters of democracy,
            73–74
        by radicals, 62–63, 64
    Cultural Revolution and, 54, 67
    economy and, 11, 12, 50, 60, 69–71,
        78
    PLA and, 60
    return to power of, 60, 67–69
    Tiananmen Square Massacre and,
        74–77
    visit to U.S., 71–72
Dismissal of Hai Rui from Office, The
    (play), 51
drugs, 16, 26
Dulles, John Foster, 62

Picture Credit

About the Author

Michael V. Uschan has written more than sixty books, including *Life of an American Soldier in Iraq*, for which he won the 2005 Council for Wisconsin Writers Juvenile Nonfiction Award. It was the second time he won the award. Mr. Uschan began his career as a writer and editor with United Press International, a wire service that provides stories to newspapers, radio, and television. Journalism is sometimes called "history in a hurry." Mr. Uschan considers writing history books a natural extension of the skills he developed in his many years as a journalist. He and his wife, Barbara, reside in the Milwaukee suburb of Franklin, Wisconsin.